Good Manners

for Every Occasion

Emilie Barnes

HARVEST HOUSE PUBLISHERS

EUGENE, OREGON

Cover by Dugan Design Group, Bloomington, Minnesota

Cover photo © Patty Calfy/iStockphoto

GOOD MANNERS FOR EVERY OCCASION
Copyright © 2008 by Emilie Barnes
Published by Harvest House Publishers
Eugene, Oregon 97402
www.harvesthousepublishers.com

Library of Congress Cataloging-in-Publication Data
  Barnes, Emilie.
  Good manners for every occasion / Emilie Barnes.
    p. cm.
  ISBN-13: 978-0-7369-2255-5 (pbk.)
  ISBN-10: 0-7369-2255-5
  1. Etiquette. I. Title.
  BJ1853.B38 2008
  395—dc22

                                                    2007028655

Printed in the United States of America

        08 09 10 11 12 13 14 15 16 / VP-SK / 11 10 9 8 7 6 5 4 3 2

FEB 0 4 2009

Dedication

This book is dedicated to one of my very favorite aunts, Auntie Evelyn. When I was eight years old, my mother, Irene, was ill and was not able to take care of me as she would have liked. She sent me to stay with my aunt for a while. Auntie Evelyn was a stickler about etiquette and manners. I'm thankful for that year I was in her home. It was like a finishing school for me. At that time in my young life, I was so shy and hated to be reprimanded. I wanted to do everything right the first time.

I am so grateful for the patience that Auntie Evelyn had with me. The skills I learned while in her home have been so valuable in my adult life. I owe it all to her. Thank you, Auntie Evelyn.

Emilie

Contents

The Joy of Manners

*Y*ou'd think that by the time people reach adulthood, they would have cultivated good manners. Simple observations would show otherwise. Somewhere along the line Mom and Dad passed over the importance of manners. Today's culture is not geared toward the development of manners. Compared to earlier decades, the current climate in the home and work place is far more casual. Kids growing up these days are a generation of "finger eaters" who are more familiar with (and inclined to want) drive-through windows than dining tables. They eat quickly and in the backseat of the car as a parent drives them to another activity. None of this is very conducive to teaching proper etiquette!

Our society hasn't placed a high priority on developing social graces. Therefore, many adults didn't grow up being taught how to be polite and gracious in various settings and circumstances. But these manners are invaluable, and the good news is that we can learn the importance of practicing social graces whether we grew up with such training or not.

The Golden Rule is really the foundation of proper etiquette and manners. It is also important for knowing how to get along at home, in business, and in social circles. Some people don't like rules growing up, but adult life is different.

Even in our home life, proper behavior creates an atmosphere of peace and harmony. Etiquette guidelines set the tone of how one treats another person with proper respect and honor. Scripture is laced with instructions regarding how a person is to properly treat others.

In earlier decades, people generally treated each other with kindness and respect. In today's culture, we don't tend to be concerned about others in our lives. We have become a "me" generation. We ask, "What's in it for me?" To have proper graces, we need to set our minds to serve the other person with kindness and respect.

Social graces are positive rules, guidelines, and cues that make it easier to interact with people and to live a day-by-day, pleasant life. If you know how to dine with others and how to introduce and meet others, you'll be more at ease and comfortable in business, social events, and your interactions with your family members. Being kind, thoughtful, and considerate will never go out of style.

Manners smooth out our rough edges of life. They civilize us. Treating people of all ages and walks of life properly is the right thing to do.

Corporations sometimes send their executives to finishing schools to learn what they didn't learn as children. It's quite normal for these companies to interview their candidates along with their wives or husbands at a fine restaurant to observe how they'll behave in various social settings. Evaluating the people skills of their potential team member is vital. Such methods are not just good manners but are excellent business practices.

This book will cover as many details of good manners as possible, including how to apply them. As you read, if your understanding of good manners improves in any way, my effort in writing will have been worthwhile.

Good manners start with following basic rules and priorities, and bad manners start with disregarding the basic rules and priorities. What could be simpler? So why does the twenty-first century seem overpopulated with young people and adults who lack basic social skills?

May this book be your source of encouragement and guidance as you enjoy the rich, generous, and abundant life that comes from embracing the best behavior for everyday living.

1

The Beginning of Manners

*You shall love the Lord your God
with all your heart and with all your
soul and with all your might.*

—Deuteronomy 6:5 NASB

Our homes are a reflection of who we are. The curb appeal from the street that reaches up to the front door will reflect or reject the statement "You are welcome here." Whether you have a condo, villa, apartment, mobile home, or a residential home, you can create an impression that says, "Come in and enjoy a cup of tea." I have a friend who lives up three flights of stairs, and at her front door she has a wreath, which she changes for each season. When you approach her apartment, you feel welcomed.

What does this have to do with manners? Manners begin at the front door and then extend into the home, where they are taught, modeled, and expressed. The pleasing home is not measured by perfection. It is measured by the foundation of gracious style you've laid. Our homes should be neat with a swept sidewalk leading to the front door. A potted flowering plant is always a welcome sign for your guests and your family. When you take care of your home, those who live there and those who visit know that they too will be cared for.

My guests love to walk into my home when something is cooking on the stove. The rich aroma of food invites the guest beyond the front door. If nothing else, try boiling a few cinnamon sticks in a pot of hot water. This will at least lead your friends to believe you are domestic.

The personality of a welcoming home makes guests want to linger, regardless of whether that home is a hut or a palace. Don't feel as if your home has to be decorated exactly the way you want it in order to express a personality that beckons with open arms. Remember, a home is always in process. If you wait to invite guests until it is the way you want it, you will never have guests. People love you for who you are and not what your home looks like.

Now may the Lord of peace himself continually
grant you peace in every circumstance.
—2 Thessalonians 3:16 nasb

A cheerful "Hello" and a "Please come in" are as welcoming as a big smile. Standing in the front doorway while having a neighborly chat says, "I don't want you in my home." Yes, a wise person must be cautious when an unknown person appears at the door. But most often the person approaching your door is a friend, neighbor, parent of one of your kid's friends, or someone else who is connected to your life in one way or another.

If you want a lesson in creating a welcoming home, the best classroom you can visit is the South. This culture has earned and deserves the "Southern hospitality" reputation. I've had the good fortune to visit Charleston, South Carolina, and Savannah, Georgia, and both cities seemed to say, "Welcome to our lifestyle." The South shines as a model of grace, charm, and hospitality. It's a place where people even slow down a bit from their hectic pace of life to enjoy the ritual of afternoon tea—one of my favorite things! This section of the country still honors social poise and presentation. Grandmother's china cups and silver elements are still reverenced in the home. The table isn't covered with plastic and paper goods. And table manners are alive and well even among the young.

The ingredients of hospitality and social graces go together regardless of where you live. You might use different elements and different languages, but wherever you are, don't forget these two ingredients.

When you entertain, practice proper etiquette and manners before you send out your invitations. People take notice and will learn from how you handle yourself in these situations. These settings are great learning situations for your children too. We all have to sharpen our social skills. At each gathering we have a chance to learn something new—something valuable to use later.

> *Enrich someone's life today with a warm word of praise. Both of you will be better for it.*
> —UNKNOWN

Etiquette IQ Test

Before we dive into the details of good manners, I encourage you to take this brief etiquette IQ test to see how much you need to learn. These few yes or no questions will help you know where your strengths are and where you need the most focused attention. Circle your answers to each question.

1. If you aren't sure of which utensil to use at a social gathering, watch the host or hostess and follow the leader.

   Yes   No

2. Talking loudly on a cell phone in a restaurant is okay.

   Yes   No

3. Before you take young children to a social event, check with the host.

   Yes   No

4. Refreshing your makeup at the dining table in a restaurant is okay.

Yes No

5. When setting the table, place the salad fork to the left of the dinner fork.

Yes No

6. Reaching for a basket of bread is okay if you don't knock over someone's glass of water.

Yes No

7. If you need to use a toothpick to clean your teeth, you should excuse yourself and go to the restroom.

Yes No

8. You should send a thank-you card when you receive a gift.

Yes No

9. Buttering all of your bread at one time is best.

Yes No

10. The dinner knife should be placed to the right of your plate with the sharp edge facing out.

Yes No

11. At the dining table, pass food to the left.

Yes No

12. Sending a thank-you note by e-mail or text message is fine.

Yes No

13. When sending out invitations to a social event, allow adequate time for the guests to respond.

Yes No

14. When leaving the table during the meal, you should place your napkin to the right of your plate.

Yes No

15. Your cell phone should always be turned off when you are at church.

    Yes   No

16. You may attend a funeral, church service, or wedding in casual attire.

    Yes   No

17. You will have to miss certain social occasions when you can't find a proper babysitter for your young children.

    Yes   No

18. Men should extend certain courtesies to ladies.

    Yes   No

19. A gentleman should not offer to shake hands with a lady until she first offers her hand to shake.

    Yes   No

20. The signal to tell your waiter that you are finished with your meal is to place your knife and fork at the nine o'clock position on your plate.

    Yes   No

Answers

1. Yes   2. No   3. Yes   4. No   5. Yes   6. No   7. Yes
8. Yes   9. No   10. No   11. No   12. No   13. Yes   14. No
15. Yes   16. No   17. Yes   18. Yes   19. Yes   20. No

Scorecard

0–5:   You really need this book. HELP!

6–10:   You need a refresher course. You didn't pay attention to Mother.

11–15:   You're on the right track, but more is to be learned.

16–18:   Your parents did a good job training you.

19–20:   Go to the head of the class. However, you'll love this book.

2

What Does *Mannerly* Mean?

Manners are the sincere, considerate, and simple expressions of important values in everyday life.

—PEGGY POST

*I*t doesn't take long to figure out if people have good manners. People who exhibit good manners are enjoyable to be around. They always seem to have an abundance of friends. These individuals express sincere warmth in their greeting and put others at ease. The kindness they exhibit on the outside reflects their inward commitment to the Golden Rule. In some fashion they share the following characteristics and values:

Tact. People who are mannerly value honesty and also realize that they needn't be brutally frank when talking with others. Speaking one's mind is not always a virtue. One must learn to set aside her own personal opinions and biases. And she must think before she acts or speaks. Remember, you never have to apologize for words you haven't spoken. A tactful person knows how easily thoughtless words or deeds can hurt others, so she guards her tongue.

Respect. We live in a very diverse world, so when in a social setting, we should respect others' rights. If we disagree with someone's opinion, we can schedule an appointment to discuss these differences in private. A well-mannered person respects differing points of view. We are to treat others as we would have others treat us.

Self-confidence. When you have a sense of social manners, you can be comfortable in all kinds of situations, even the unexpected ones. A confident person knows how to interact in most social and business situations and has the confidence to communicate with others even in demanding or difficult circumstances. In other words, confidence enables grace to exist under pressure. Have you been around very confident people? They seem to inspire confidence in others because they aren't worried about their every move and comment and decision. They are very positive and often direct in their approach to life. You seldom hear them concentrate on the negative aspects of life, and those around them follow suit. Confidence is infectious.

Flexibility. A mannerly person understands that etiquette is an expression of cultural and social values. We would expect that people from the Southern states might do things one way, and people from the West Coast might be more flexible in their customs. One must learn to modify or change her manners to accommodate the traditions of other countries and cultures. This doesn't mean you stop being on your best behavior—it means that you should observe the climate you are in and respect their standards before you act and speak.

Common sense. One would think that common sense would be common, but that doesn't seem to be the case anymore. People who are mannerly know how to facilitate good relations with others by adapting to the needs of others without sacrificing their own values. This person knows how to choose her battles while also understanding that all battles aren't worth the fight. Good manners don't limit anyone's ability to act boldly or to think deeply; instead, they permit people to disagree agreeably.

A person who reflects these traits can function very well in all kinds of situations and settings. These characteristics are most important in everyday relationships and within families, where respectful and considerate behavior cements the bond of love and affection.

Thankfully, we can learn good manners at any age, but when the learning process begins in childhood, mannerly behavior becomes more natural. Parents, that's why it's so important to begin teaching good manners when your children are young. It's always easier to prevent bad habits from being formulated than to try and correct bad behaviors that have already become habits. An early start takes advantage of a child's instinct to learn.

Manners are the happy ways of doing things.

—RALPH WALDO EMERSON

~ 3~

Entertaining at Home

The homeliest tasks get beautiful
if loving hands do them.

—Louisa May Alcott

America has nearly abandoned the idea of entertaining at home. Restaurants have become the backdrop where many people entertain business peers and socialize with friends. You will often hear all kinds of excuses why they don't entertain at home:

- I'm too busy to entertain.
- Dining out is cheaper than preparing food at home.
- The young children prevent me from having guests at home.
- My apartment, condo, mobile home, or house is too small.
- I don't have the proper serving dishes.
- I can't find good help to assist me.
- I don't have a clue how to properly entertain.
- I'm not very good in the kitchen.
- I can't seem to coordinate all the elements of entertaining so it all comes together at the same time.

At one time or another we've all uttered one of these excuses—maybe even a few of them. However, for every reason against entertaining at home, there is a rebuttal. I believe a lot of the arguments are born out of a misunderstanding of what entertaining truly is—people envision a huge gala or a very elegant evening with detailed menus, fancy decorations, and hired servers. This would be delightful, but it is only one version of entertaining, and it's intimidating. You're entertaining when you invite a small group over for book club. You're entertaining when you have an elderly neighbor over for a cup of tea and a scone. You're entertaining when you host a barbeque for the neighborhood in your backyard. And you're entertaining when you have six other couples over for an evening dinner. In each case you've taken the time and effort to invite people to your home for a meal. For all the effort you expend to entertain, you'll be blessed by what you get back in return.

Don't say, "I can't do that." Just do it! I want this book to inspire you and provide you with the basic skills you need as you start out on this new journey. You do not need to follow high-society rules and regulations to become an effective host. However, there are some traditional tried and true ways of doing things, including how to invite people, how to set the table, how to serve the food, and more.

If you need reasons to entertain, here's a good one: We need to be around other people. Loneliness and isolation are two big problems in the American society. We want to connect with others, yet we often choose to be alone. People go to work, come home, close the garage door, and don't come out until the next day when they start the same routine over—day after day, week after week, month after month.

Entertaining will help you get out of your rut and routine so that you can experience the joy of being with other people. Sometimes you'll be a host, and other times you'll be a guest. Proper etiquette will enrich your life as you embrace both roles.

It's Easy
Entertaining is bringing two or more people together for a general reason. It might be a small, medium, or large gathering. If you haven't

done a lot of entertaining, make it easy on yourself and start small. Don't get caught up in too many plans, especially in the beginning. Decide on a day to do something with someone and stick to it. It really is that easy. You can gather people simply by saying something like this:

- "Come on over after church on Sunday for a brunch."
- "Come over on Friday afternoon at four to have a cup of tea."
- "I'm giving an omelet and waffle party for our committee on Saturday morning at nine thirty, and I'd love for you to come."
- "Everyone in the neighborhood wants to view our newly decorated home, so we're having an open house this Sunday from two to four. Light refreshments will be served. We'd love to see you."
- "Our daughter is having her tenth birthday party on Tuesday after school starting at four. She'd be delighted to have your daughter, Mary, attend. We hope she can come."
- "Our big Fourth of July swim party is just around the corner. Your whole family is invited to join us for fun, food, and games."

The best guest list includes a mixture of people you know that have diversified backgrounds and interest. This uncommonness makes for such an interesting occasion. Remember, to make entertaining special, don't worry about what you don't have. What you do with what you have is much more important.

Extending invitations to others is fun and very rewarding. It takes so little to be above average. Get the whole family involved in your entertaining process. Your efforts and attitude will be a great model for your children when they're on their own and are ready to have parties and gatherings. Mom and Dad's example becomes their foundation.

Welcome is what reflects God's spirit
of love, joy, and happiness.

—EMILIE BARNES

Spontaneous Entertaining

It's very satisfying to throw an event complete with written invitations, elaborate decorations, and lavish foods. Hosting a very formal dinner overflowing with the spirit of loveliness is very fulfilling. Sharing your most beautiful tablecloths, place settings, and centerpieces can be so enjoyable. Such nice touches certainly show guests that you spent time, attention, and care preparing for their visit.

And yet we rob ourselves of much joy when we limit our entertaining to what we can arrange in advance. We'll enrich our lives when we get in the habit of spur-of-the-moment hospitality. I don't mean that you'll invite 12 people over for a seven-course meal on a whim. But there are so many times when extending an in-the-moment invitation to someone is exactly what you want to do, but you hesitate because you aren't sure if you'd have what you need to host even a casual get-together. When you start talking to a neighbor out at the mailboxes, it'd be nice to invite her in for tea. While at the grocery store, if you see a friend who has been going through a hard time, you'd like to ask her to follow you home and have lunch with you.

Robert Louis Stevenson said, "A friend is a present you give yourself." Planning for spontaneous entertaining is one of the most important ways of giving that gift. Friendships are cultivated through spending time together. So purposely plan to make that happen, whether the actual event is planned or not.

I treasure the memories of impromptu parties. They've been times of great cheer and new friendships. But these are almost always more successful with a bit of advance planning. Advance planning to be spontaneous? That's right. A certain amount of thinking ahead will make spontaneous events possible, or at least widen the possibilities for spontaneous at-home celebrations. I don't want you to miss out on

one more chance to develop a friendship or to reach out to someone in need of fellowship.

Planning to Be Spontaneous

What holds you back from inviting someone into your house for a visit? Is it your décor? The state of cleanliness? Your lack of groceries or washed napkins? Do you cringe at the thought of the bills and school papers that are spread out all over your dining room table and decide against opening the door wide with a welcoming spirit?

Flowers, silk or real, and a pretty vase on hand mean that you'll always have something ready for a centerpiece. If you set aside room in your freezer for frozen casseroles and appetizers, you'll always have something ready to serve in a pinch. And if you spend efficient, daily time tidying and putting everything in its place, your house will always be clean enough for an impromptu celebration. Stock those cupboards with plates, napkins, and flatware so when the time comes, you'll be ready.

What you keep on hand will truly save the day and open up your life to more celebrations and times of fellowship. Here's a basic list of items that are good to have in your home. With any combination of these you can make a walk-in visitor feel like a king or queen.

Bisquick	brownie mix
tea—regular and herb	coffee—regular and decaffeinated
eggs	butter
sour cream	flour
sugar	yellow cake mix
vanilla instant pudding	brown sugar
raisins	nuts
canned fruit cocktail	shredded coconut
muffins	graham cracker crumbs

chocolate chips	marshmallows
cinnamon	nutmeg
sweetened condensed milk	frozen berries
frozen pound cake	frozen juice
frozen bread dough	ready-made pie crusts
refrigerator biscuits	

You'll be surprised at how many wonderful opportunities to entertain will present themselves when you're prepared. You'll welcome people into your heart and your home with more eagerness and ease.

*Be kindly affectionate to one another with
brotherly love, in honor giving preference
to one another. . .given to hospitality.*

—ROMANS 12:10-13 NKJV

The Art of Invitations

Make new friends and keep the old,
One is silver and the other gold.

Most Americans have become very casual in their approach to inviting someone to a dinner party. Casual seems to be a fashion statement in Southern California. However, certain occasions call for a more formal approach when inviting your guests. Such an invitation might look like this:

> *Dear Jennifer,*
>
> *Will you and Bill come to dinner at our home on Friday, November 3, at 6:30 p.m.?*
>
> *We hope that you are able to come.*
>
> *With love,*
>
> *Emilie*

An informal note of invitation is usually sent out about a week before the set date. Invitations to very close friends may be sent only three days in advance. Formal invitations are sent from ten days to three weeks in advance. Remember that everyone has busy calendars—so "the sooner, the better" is a good rule of thumb if you want people to come. Formal invitations use the same form whether they're written or engraved.

Most communities have stores that specialize in composing and printing your invitations for a very reasonable price. These stores have a great selection of theme papers, cards, and envelopes that make a statement when they arrive at your honored guest's home.

The Informal Note of Acceptance or Regret

> *Dear Emilie,*
>
> *Bill and I would love to join you for dinner on Friday night at 6:30.*
>
> *We look forward to seeing you again.*
>
> *Lovingly,*
>
> *Jennifer*

> *Dear Emilie,*
>
> *Bill and I are so sorry that we won't be able to have dinner with you on Friday evening as we have a previous engagement. Thank you so much for thinking of us.*
>
> *Let's try again soon.*
>
> *Sincerely,*
>
> *Jennifer*

It's perhaps needless to say that acceptance or regrets must be sent at once so that the hostess may know how many to expect or how many other guests to invite. Of the two, regrets must be sent out sooner, for the hostess needs all the time she can get to invite someone else.

Every invitation should be replied to within a week. A host needs to know possible problems with the invited guests' schedule. When you're invited to an event, always RSVP by the timeline presented and never be a no-show if you've committed to attending.

Invitation by Telephone

For some informal occasions, you can call your guests at the last moment. We often find that these last-minute invitations fit into our busy schedule. Never use the telephone to invite someone to a more formal engagement.

Some invitations might ask for you to RSVP by phone. If so, a formal acceptance or note of regret would not be necessary. In this case you could call and tell your hostess of your plans. Even though e-mails have worked their way into how people correspond, I would not recommend this method of corresponding.

The Last-Minute Invitation and Reply

When the occasion arises to replace a person at the last minute, you may call upon a close friend to fill the vacancy. Invitations would ideally match the others if time permits sending a note, but most likely they are made by telephone, personally, or by word of mouth through some member of the family. The reply must be made at once.

How good and pleasant it is when
brothers live together in unity.
—Psalm 133:1

Homemade Invitations

Here's an easy and elegant homemade invitation that you can adapt to a number of occasions. For each invitation, you'll need a heavy sheet of 8½ by 11–inch paper. You'll also need a pencil, scissors or a craft knife, gold and silver paint pens with a medium or wide point, a fine-point pen in blue or black, and a small piece of cardboard to make a template. If you want to mail the invitations, you'll need to purchase envelopes large enough to hold a 4¼ by 5½–inch card.

To make the invitation, fold the sheet of paper in half, bringing the short edges together, and then fold in half again. You should now have a folded 4¼ x 5½–inch card. Position it so that it opens like a book in front of you—with open edges at right and bottom. Mark the front or top surface of the card very lightly with a pencil. Open up the paper, which is now marked by the folds into rectangles, and look for the rectangle you marked. Trace a 4-inch oval onto a piece of cardboard, cut it out to make a template, center it on the front rectangle, and trace around it. Carefully cut out this oval with scissors or a craft knife, and then refold the card so that the front has an oval "window." With a pencil, lightly trace around the window onto the next layer of paper. Then use the silver and gold paint pens to draw a wavy "picture frame" around the oval, alternating scalloped silver and gold lines until the "frame" is about ½-inch thick. Outline the frame with blue or black fine-tip pen and draw in alternating silver and gold lines behind the frame to suggest striped wallpaper. If you wish, add lines at top to suggest an old-fashioned wire picture hanger.

Open the card once more and find the oval you penciled in. Place the cardboard template over it, matching the edges to the penciled lines, and trace around the template with a black or blue fine-point pen. Use the same pen to write the little "silver and gold" poem found at the beginning of this chapter. When you refold the card once more, the poem should appear in the frame. Then open the card like a book and write your actual invitation inside.[1]

~ 5 ~

Company Manners

There is no place in the world where
courtesy is so necessary as in the home.

—HELEN HATHAWAY

*Y*our evening dinner time is a wonderful chance to practice "company" manners with your family. Mom, they don't all have to be taught in a single setting. Before we discuss the company manners, I want to emphasize the importance of what we call "teachable moments" around our home. Consider Deuteronomy 6:6-7:

> And these words which I command you today shall be in your heart. You shall teach them diligently to your children, and shall talk of them when you sit in your house, when you walk by the way, when you lie down, and when you rise up (NKJV).

These verses encourage parents to use every opportunity to teach these values that are important to us down to the next generation. A dear, gentle mother and a kind, firm father are the main influences in our homes. Not the neighbors, not the schools, not the church, but the people inside the four walls that we call home. As women, we help our husbands set the thermostat of our homes. Proverbs 31:26-27 states, "When she speaks, her words are wise, and kindness is the rule for everything she says. She watches carefully all that goes on throughout her household and is never lazy" (TLB).

Several of the biggest time wasters in your home are the telephone, cell phone, TV, and computer technology. We must be aware of these time wasters so that they don't consume the time that should be spent teaching our children. Harmony, kindness, and worship of the Lord are ever so important in the home where good manners are a constant aim. We teach a little at a time over a long period of time.

If we want to raise responsible children, we need to give them responsibilities (chores). Mom and Dad have to be good examples around the home. Children will usually mirror the behavior that the adults exhibit. Back to the dinner table scenario, if we eat with our fingers, so will they. Yes, there are certain foods that would be eaten with their fingers, such as sandwiches, ice cream cones, spare ribs, pizza, dips, and chips. (My Bob says that fried chicken is also on the list. He comes from Texas, and he insists on having that margin of error.)

As the host, you can set your family and guests at ease by informing them that certain foods may be eaten with their fingers if they wish. If so, provide a cup with warm water and a hand wipe so that they can wash and wipe their fingers when finished eating.

Cherish these times around the table. Take it slow and easy. Offer plenty of time for conversation. Intentionally slow down the pace. While you're demonstrating manners for your children, you can review the company manners needed for an upcoming evening of guests. These are a few that might be relevant to your gathering:

Before Your Guests Arrive

- Be ready at least 30 minutes before your guests are expected to arrive. Nothing is more awkward for the guests than watching the host run around and tidy up.
- If you have children, make sure all their toys are picked up from the rooms that you and your company will be using.

- Fluff the sofa pillows, but don't place them where your guests won't feel like messing them up.

- The evening will go a lot smoother if you've planned ahead of time for special touches. If it's wintertime, have logs on hand for a fire.

- Be sure to put out a fresh bar of soap, guest towels, and a scented candle in the bathroom to be used by visitors.

- Have umbrellas handy in case it rains so that departing guests can get to their cars without getting wet.

Ding-Dong: When the Guests Arrive

- Properly greet guests at the door.

- Assist in taking any coats or purses, putting them all in an easy location.

- Introduce guests to the rest of the family—make sure everyone knows each other.

- Offer them something to drink.

- Escort them to the living room and offer them a place to sit.

- Have place cards present on the dining room table so your company will know where to sit.

- Prearrange the placement of your guests around the table so strangers will get to know others easily.

- If you are serving the food, remember to serve from the left and remove plates from the right.

- Napkins should be opened and placed in your lap.

- Remember to wipe your mouth and fingers after drinking and eating.

- Take medium to small bites when eating, chew your food well, and don't speak with food in your mouth.

- Elbows must not be on the edge of the table while eating.

These are only a few of the guidelines for making company feel at home, but they'll give some order to your event. Other adults love to see your children included in the evening's activities. And they really love to see your children well-behaved. However, there are times when you'll have an adults-only dinner. A child can still be a part of the evening by greeting the guests and even helping to serve meals and clear the table.

In an appropriate situation, you might want to offer a toast or a prayer before the meal. After all, thankful people do give thanks. Here are a couple of examples:

To God who gives us daily bread,
A thankful song we raise,
And pray that He who sends us food
Will fill our hearts with praise. Amen.

As we now from our bounty eat,
Keep us humble, kind, and sweet,
May we serve Thee, Lord, each day
And feel Thy love, dear Lord, we pray.

Come, dear Lord,
Be our guest and become our host.
Be pleased to bless this food
And us who dwell here. Amen.

Other Table Manners for Both Host and Guest

- The gentlemen are to pull out the chairs for the ladies and help them to be seated.
- The napkin is put on your lap with folded side toward your waist.
- Watch the head of the table to see what to do next.

- The honored guest is the first to be served and the lady to the left will be served next.

- Proceed around the table until all have been served. The host is the last to be served.

- Any dirty utensil should go beside the plate—soup spoons can be left in the soup bowl.

- You are permitted to use your fingers to pick up the bread. Cut or tear up the bread in small parts that you would eat at one time. Only butter that small portion one at a time.

- Bread plates are placed to the left of the dinner plate.

- Have servings of butter, salt, and pepper at each end of the table for ease of passing.

- If you must leave the table after being seated, excuse yourself and place your napkin on your chair.

- Never hurry your meal—these are precious times together.

- After everyone has eaten and the conversation has been sweet, the host might politely ask everyone to move into the living room where the sofas and chairs are more comfortable.

Having company provides a wonderful opportunity for old friends and new friends to come together. It's also a great time for the whole family to review a few of the important manners so your family puts its best foot forward.

Life be not so short but that there
is always time for courtesy.

—RALPH WALDO EMERSON

Tips on Tipping

Give and it shall be given unto you.

—LUKE 6:38

*O*ur society is becoming more and more a service population. Tipping is a way we can say thank you to people for providing service to us. The amount of tip is always one open to discussion—it should equal the amount of your satisfaction for their service. In America a tip of 15 to 20 percent of the bill before taxes is a good guideline.

Below are some tipping guidelines that one can use to determine what is appropriate.

Eating Out

When dining out, the typical tip to leave is 15 percent, but if the service has been exceptional or if you have lingered at the table longer than usual, consider 20 percent. If you have received poor service or rudeness on the part of the server, you may want to talk to the owner or manager of the restaurant.

- Tip the coat attendant one to two dollars.
- Tip the valet who parks your car one to two dollars—often they will have the charges posted. The posted sign is to the valet service, but it doesn't include a tip for the attendant.
- Tip the musicians, if available, one to two dollars. If several

songs are played especially for you and your guests, consider five dollars.

- Tip the restroom attendant 50 cents to a dollar. Often there is a bowl there to place your tip.

- When eating at a cafeteria or buffet, no tipping is required. However, if a waiter brings you drinks and removes plates, consider leaving a 10 percent tip at the table.

- Food servers on average make about half of their income from gratuities. Often your tip is pooled and distributed among employees including the maître d', the bus boy, and the dishwasher.[1]

Beauty Salons and Spas
- hairdresser—15 percent (If the stylist or hairdresser is the owner of the business, a tip is not necessary.)
- manicurists—$2.00
- shampooists—$2.00
- masseuse—10 to 20 percent

Hotel
- bellhop—$2.00 for the first bag and $1.00 for each additional bag he handles
- concierge—If they are able to arrange good sporting events or concert tickets, you might want to tip around $5.00.
- housekeeping staff—It is best to leave a little something in an envelope each night instead of a larger amount prior to checkout as several different workers may be attending to the room during the week.

Airport
Redcaps mostly work on tips for their income. You should tip a

dollar per bag for this service. You need not pay the airline desk handler if you check in inside the airport.

Other Services

During the holidays you may consider tipping those service people who work for you such as paper deliverers, cleaning ladies, and gardeners. Mail carriers can't accept cash, but they can accept gifts up to $20 in value. Remember, we all like to feel appreciated. The amount of the tip depends upon your value of their services.

Presenting tips in person is the best way to show your appreciation. This way you can say, "Thank you!"

It is more blessed to give than to receive.
—ACTS 20:35

~ 7 ~

Passing On Your Values

A man is never so tall as when
he stoops to help a child.

—Abraham Lincoln

Couples should discuss which values they want to pass on to their children. One of the great joys of having children is to be able to pass on to the next generation those values that we feel are useful and necessary for a good life. We're not here on earth just to have fun and be friends with our offspring. As parents, we are to be teachers to our children. Being a parent includes a lot of responsibilities. It isn't easy. Tough love is…tough.

The values you teach and model will become the foundation for your child's manners and etiquette. Take a hard look at the values you want to pass on. Mom and Dad will need to compromise and agree on these values. Presenting and modeling two different sets of values (Mom's and Dad's) will confuse the child.

If you've never done this before, take time to define and clarify these values. Below is a list of values you might consider:

- religious beliefs
- family importance

- good manners
- honorable behavior with good character
- generosity
- respect for ethnic and cultural differences
- self-discipline
- work ethics
- service to the community
- honesty and integrity
- loyalty and reliability
- good sportsmanship
- good financial skills
- value of marriage
- respect for authority
- an understanding of right and wrong

Once you've made your list, take the time to rank them in priority of importance. As husband and wife, you may have different rankings, but try to agree on the first five or six virtues. It's okay to disagree, but attempt to agree on the basic few.

All major cultures and religions have their version of the Golden Rule, which tells us to treat others as we would like to be treated (see Luke 6:31). This is the core value of good manners and good etiquette. It requires that we have an understanding of other people and their needs.

Practicing good manners in our everyday life is very important. Our children will learn by watching what we do. These are some of the ways we can mentor our children:

- Show empathy. Empathy is the capacity to understand how others feel, to walk in their shoes. We should encourage and praise our children when we see them have empathy for another person or a pet. If empathy isn't encouraged, it may wither away. To develop this part of a child's behavior, take time to discuss feelings with your child. At a very young age, a child can identify emotional feelings such as these: happy, glad, angry, bored, sad, scared, and so on.

- Encourage your child to see how people of different backgrounds act, speak, and live. People from different cultures, religions, and value systems may respond differently than we do. Take time to talk about these differences. Their values may not necessarily be wrong—just different from ours.

- Praise your children when they are considerate to others. Continually be on the lookout for opportunities to praise children for good behavior. Positive reinforcement will encourage the child to do the same thing again without being told or asked to do so.

- Be concerned about others. Since you're the pacesetter in your children's lives, they will be influenced by what they see you doing. If you're empathetic to others, they'll also follow your lead. If you find a lost wallet on the sidewalk and attempt to locate the owner so you can return the missing wallet to its rightful owner, you'll have an opportunity to discuss what's right in such a situation. Your children can learn many lessons of character development when they see you behaving in the right way.

- Practice what you preach. Children will see through you if your walk is different from your talk. Those little eyes have a wide-angle lens. They are watching so carefully to see how you respond to various conflicts that arise in your family's life. How do you respond to the policeman when he gives you a ticket for speeding? Are you able to forgive those who offend you? Can you control the tone of your voice when you're angry? Are you able to apologize to someone when you are wrong in a certain situation?

The hardest job kids face today is learning
good manners without seeing any.

—FRED ASTAIRE

~ 8 ~

Table Manners

The ideal guest is an equally ideal hostess; the
principle of both is the same; a quick sympathy,
a happy outlook, and consideration for others.

—EMILY POST, *ETIQUETTE*

Often we think that good table manners are for the benefit of our home life only. But the practice of table manners establishes habits that carry far beyond a meal at the dining table. The home front is the training ground for adult life behaviors, traditions, and values. Good table manners and social skills can mean the difference in a hiring or promotion in your career and in the future careers of your children.

Good etiquette becomes a lifestyle. You don't just put it on to impress people and then go back to your crude behavior when someone isn't watching. It's a natural part of who you are. When you know and practice good behavior, you are at ease in all kinds of social settings, including small gatherings or big company functions. You'll be much more at ease when you know a few basic principles, such as what fork to use and when it's okay to begin eating.

Let's first look at how to set a table and then how to use the table setting properly. If you know the road map, you won't be surprised or awkward when you begin dining. If you are ever in doubt, watch what the hosts do and follow their actions. If you're the host, these next sections will be very helpful to you.

The Silver Setting

An easy way to remember which utensil to use is to work your way in on both sides.

Formal Dinner

A. napkin

B. service plate

C. soup bowl on a liner plate

D. bread and butter plate with butter knife

E. water glass

F. red wine glass

G. white wine glass

H. fish fork

I. dinner fork

J. salad fork

K. dessert fork

L. knife

M. fish knife

N. teaspoon

O. soup spoon

Luncheon

A. napkin

B. luncheon plate

C. soup (or other first course plate) on a liner plate

D. bread and butter plate with butter knife

E. water glass

F. wine glass

G. luncheon fork

H. knife

I. teaspoon

J. soup spoon

Buffet Setting

This is how to set a buffet:

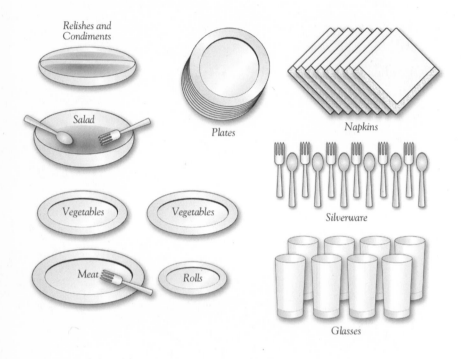

Relishes and Condiments

Salad

Plates

Napkins

Vegetables   Vegetables

Silverware

Meat   Rolls

Glasses

Man does not live by bread alone.

—Deuteronomy 8:3

Silverware

The proper placement of your silverware signals to the server at what stage of the meal you are. If you pause for a breather, place the utensils in the resting position. This signals that you aren't finished yet and that you plan to continue your meal.

Resting Position

Finished Position

When you are finished, place your utensils at the 4:00 position. It tells your server that you're finished and that he can remove your plate from the table.

Proper Seating

Depending on the mix of the gathering, the host is seated at one end of the table and the hostess at the other end. A male honored guest sits to the right of the hostess, and if the honored guest is a female, she is seated to the right of the host. Balance the rest of the guests male, female, male, female.

Table Courtesies

At all times observe what the host does. Wait for the hostess to be seated before you sit down. The man will assist the lady to his right to be seated first. After she's been seated, the gentleman may take his seat. Wait for the host to indicate in word or by action that it's okay to begin eating. In some settings, someone may offer a prayer of thanksgiving or a toast to the honored guest.

Order of the Menu

The number of courses offered depends on how formal the dinner is. Most offerings will be five courses.

1. The appetizer or hors d'oeuvre. This course might be as simple as nuts or cheese and crackers offered in the living room before dinner.

2. Soup or fish. The host will plan from a wide variety of offerings.

3. Salad. Keep the serving small.

4. Entrée. This is the main course. It will consist of meats, fish, pasta, or poultry with an offering of vegetables and a starch.

5. Dessert with hot beverage. Most people today are very health conscious and tend to watch their calories. Make available a wide selection of teas and coffees. Fruit slices and an assortment of cheeses are healthy options.

Napkin

Watch the host to see when you should unfold your napkin. As soon as the host does so, that is a signal for you to do likewise. Here are a couple of reminders regarding the placement and use of the napkin:

- If the guests wear black clothing, you might want to offer black napkins so the white linen napkins don't leave lint on their clothing.

- Unfold the napkin to the half-folded position and place in your lap with the centerfold against your waistline.

- If you leave the table during the meal, leave your napkin on the seat of the chair. This signals to the server that you'll be returning.

- Placing your napkin to the right of your plate indicates that you're finished with your meal. The napkin need not be folded.

- Blot your mouth after drinking and eating during the meal.

Place Cards

Including place cards on the table is very nice. They're usually put above the dinner plate at each person's place. Some hostesses put them on top of the napkin on the dinner plate. The place card is usually plain white, about an inch and a half high by two inches long. There's no exact size recommended. Use your best penmanship to print your guest's name on the card.

The place card is also helpful for people to locate where they'll be seated. If you have people who may not know each other, place cards can be helpful to remind those sitting beside them of their first name. Even after proper introductions have been made, it's easy to forget a new name.

If you'd like to add a personal touch for an upcoming event, try making the homemade place cards described in this chapter.

When to Leave the Table

Watch for the host to arise and offer for the guests to go to the living room, where additional coffees and teas may be served. One normally doesn't leave the party until the honored guest has left. At that time, the other guests may be excused. If there is no honored guest or if the honored guest is spending the night at the home of the host, the guests may feel free to excuse themselves for the evening at their appropriate time. Be careful not to stay too late in the evening.

Gifts for the Host

It's always appropriate to bring a gift for the host when you are invited to be a guest in their home. It need not be extravagant, but it may be something to let them know that you are so appreciative of them inviting you to their function. Flowers, books, music, and candies make lovely gifts for your host.

One who is gracious to a poor man lends to the Lord, and He will repay him for his good deed.
—Proverbs 19:17 NASB

Tidbits to Remember

- "As the ships sail out to sea, I spoon my soup away from me."
- When you are asked to pass the salt, pass the pepper too.
- Avoid placing your elbows on the table, and never hunch over and "hug" your plate.
- When serving food, be sure that all your guests are served first before serving yourself.
- Food should always be passed to the right (counterclockwise).
- Leaving food on your plate is not good manners.
- Cutting up your salad into bite-size pieces is up to you. You may or you may not.
- Blot your lipstick before you begin to eat your meal. You don't want to leave behind a trail of red on your dinner napkin. If you want to touch up your lipstick after a meal, it's best to excuse yourself from the table.
- If you happen to find a fish bone in your mouth, remove the bone from your mouth as discreetly possible and place it on the side of the plate.

- Lemon seeds, olive pits, and watermelon seeds do not go into your napkin but are best placed in the palm of your hand and set on the side of your plate.

- If you find food lodged between your teeth, very politely excuse yourself from the table. Take care of the problem in private and then return to the table.

- If an unexpected sneeze comes upon you at the table and you have no handkerchief or tissue available, go ahead and sneeze. But when it happens, be sure to turn your head away from the food and the guests. After the fact, a tissue or your napkin is a reassuring gesture, but when you blow, don't honk.

> *If you doubt you can accomplish something,*
> *then you can't accomplish it. You have to*
> *have confidence in your ability, and then*
> *be tough enough to follow through.*
> —ROSALYNN CARTER

Homemade Place Cards

These salt dough place cards are fun to make and a joy to present to friends and family at a gathering. Follow the recipe and invite loved ones to a time of fellowship, conversation, and the pleasures of friendship.

    2 cups flour

    1 cup salt

    ½ cup to 1 cup water

Mix flour and salt. Add water a tablespoon at a time until mixture forms a kneadable dough. Turn out onto a lightly floured surface and knead for about ten minutes. Roll out to a ⅜–inch thickness. Use cookie cutters to cut dough into desired shapes—a teapot would be especially cute for place cards. In addition, for each two place cards, cut a 2 by 4–inch rectangle out of the rolled dough. Cut the rectangle from corner to corner to make two long triangles. These will be the props that hold the place cards upright. Place the cutouts on a cookie sheet and bake in a very low oven (150 to 200 degrees) until completely hard—at least several hours. When the dough has cooled completely, paint the place cards with acrylic paint and then paint the guest's name on top. Let paint dry—then spray front and back with several layers of polyurethane varnish. Spray the triangular cutouts as well. When all is dry, use a hot-glue gun to attach the two-inch edge of the triangle to the bottom of the place cards.

If you want the place cards to lean back slightly, experiment with the shape of the prop. If you trim the 2-inch edge at a little more of an angle, the place card will lean back just a bit, showing off the name and graciously inviting friends to the table.

Manners with the Pen

Write them on the tablet of your heart.

—Proverbs 3:3

Going out to meet the letter carrier is one of the exciting times of my day. I get to receive notes and letters from my friends, and I also get to bid goodbye to the notes and letters I'm sending off to my friends. Written correspondence is becoming a lost art. We're so busy, we can't take time from our schedules. We let e-mails and text messages take the place of penning letters with a personal touch.

Something happens when I open an envelope addressed to me and read the sweet words that unfold before my eyes and heart. What wonderful medicine for my spirit. I encourage you to continue expressing yourself with written correspondence. It enriches your spirit and also heals the heart of the one who receives your words.

When my family asks me what I would like for my special occasions, I always request stationery. One can never have enough note cards. They come in all sizes, shapes, colors, and designs. Setting aside time to catch up on my correspondence is a peaceful experience. Here are some thoughts to keep in mind as you exercise this style and form of staying in touch with your friends.

- *A proper greeting.* We live in a very casual time in how we address someone, but until you get to know someone in a personal fashion, you should start out your letter with a more formal salutation, such as Mr., Mrs., or Ms. A little decorum never hurts. You'll always be safe if you err on the side of politeness. Always handwrite a formal social note.

- *Neatness.* You may be able to read your writing, but put yourself in the reader's situation. Slow down and make sure your reader will be able to decode your curves and slants. Penmanship is not a strong curriculum subject anymore in our schools. We've copped out by using the computer.

    The overall appearance of your letter tells the reader a lot about you. Coffee stains, crossed out words, misspelled words, and words too small to read give the reader the wrong impression. If you take the time to write a note, take the time to present it in a worthy fashion.

- *Be yourself.* Your writing style can and should be your own. If you are writing a personal and informal note, use natural language. You don't have to be formal and stiff if the occasion doesn't call for that style of writing. Don't use twenty-dollar words when a ten-dollar word is just as appropriate. However, in a more formal and business setting, be more businesslike. It's okay to write like you speak. People want to hear from the real you.

- *Business style.* Historically, business letters have always been typed. Any business letter is best received typed, but if you don't have the proper tools, you could write your letter in longhand. If you choose to use the handwritten format, you need to take great care to make your writing as readable as possible. Be as brief as possible.

    Be sure to always include the addressee's name and full title in addition to the company name and address. The handwritten style suggests a more casual relationship, but the wording and use of words should remain professional. If your letter has a negative message, remember that the recipient reading it is a person and treat them with the utmost respect.

Try to use clear thoughts and stay away from clunky and dull language.

- *E-mails.* I refuse to use e-mails in place of a social or personal style of saying thank you to a person. I realize that we live in a high-tech culture and that we are all busy. E-mails are great for what they are designed to do, and that is communicating in an impersonal way in business or in an emergency. Try to stay away from using this medium when you are communicating with a friend. The typed page doesn't have the heart of the handwritten word.

- *In the office.* E-mail should always be professional when corresponding to someone in the office. Make sure your e-mail is well written before you hit the Send button. An e-mail is like speech: Once it has been sent, it can't be called back.

  Keep in mind that your e-mail can be sent to other personnel and can be stored and retrieved at a future date—even to be used against you.

- *At home.* Hours are spent each day by millions of people receiving and sending out off-colored jokes and stories. Each of these communicates the sender's value standards—they reflect who you are. Discard those e-mails that don't reflect who you are and most definitely don't send smut that would not reflect your moral values. Don't be downgraded by sending out questionable material. Share with your children the proper skills for using e-mail.

*I therefore, the prisoner in the Lord, beg you
to lead a life worthy of the calling to which you
have been called, with all humility and gentleness,
with patience, bearing with one another in love.*
—Ephesians 4:1-2 NRSV

~ 10 ~

Restaurant Manners as the Host

*All the beautiful sentiments in the world
weigh less than a single lovely action.*

—JAMES RUSSELL LOWELL

How often do we say to someone as we exit our conversation, "Let's do lunch someday!" If we leave it at that, we'll probably never make it happen. Before you say it, make sure you mean it. As quickly as possible, call that friend and set a date, a time, and a place. Put it on your calendar and plan to keep your commitment.

Here are some guiding principles to observe when you're dining at a restaurant for a social or business reason:

- Be very specific about the date, time, and place when you extend your invitation.

- Since you're the one doing the inviting, it's your responsibility to pay the bill. The invitee always pays unless there are previous arrangements. Make sure this arrangement is clear before you go to a restaurant.

- Select a restaurant that is close to your guest's home or business. Check out what kind of food is served. Make sure that the food is pleasing to your guest. (Check to see if there are any dietary considerations.)

- Call your guest the afternoon before or the morning of the date to reconfirm the plans. If the meeting is important, call the restaurant to make your wishes known about your choice of table. It's no fun getting to the restaurant only to discover that they don't have your reservation.

- If you must cancel the date, call the guest personally to set a new date. Don't have a third party do the calling for you.

- Arrive at the restaurant a few minutes before the appointed time. Check the table that you have requested to make sure it is acceptable. Never be late—it is not proper to keep your guest waiting for you, the host.

- Let your guest have the best seat. If there's beautiful scenery such as the snow-capped mountains or the beauty of the waves hitting the sand, your consideration will certainly be appreciated.

- If you're familiar with the restaurant, you might make certain meal recommendations. If both of you are new to the location, you might ask your waiter to give certain recommendations.

- If your guest is served first, encourage her to begin eating while her food is hot. If your order arrives first, wait until your guest is served before you begin eating.

- Be alert to your guest's facial and body language during the meal. If something seems not right, you might ask, "Is there anything wrong?" or, "May I call the waiter over?" Some guests might be bashful about a piece of meat that needs to be cooked a little longer.

- If your guest answers, "No, no problem," do not press the issue. Some guests don't want to make a fuss.

- Depending upon the reason for the meal, you might want to talk casually before you arrive at the reason you invited the person to meet with you. If it's a social reason, you might have casual conversation throughout the meal, but if your purpose is businesslike, keep casual talk to ten to fifteen minutes and then get down to business.

- If you're having a problem with the service or food, it's better to make this evaluation away from your guest's presence. You can excuse yourself politely and go talk to the manager of the establishment. In some cases you may want to wait until you get back home or at your office before you respond to the management.

- After you've dined and have had a chance to discuss your business and take care of any details for a future meeting, you can politely stand up to signal that the meeting is over. Thank the person for coming and exit together.

You can't build a reputation on what you're going to do.
—Henry Ford

~ 11 ~

Restaurant Manners as the Guest

It is good to have an end to journey towards;
But it is the journey that matters, in the end.

—URSULA K. LEGUIN

The proper etiquette of the guest is as important as that of the host. Sometimes we are hosts, and sometimes we are guests. We don't always have to take the lead—it takes a wise person to know the difference. You may like to control the situation and enjoy being the host, but sometimes you must be willing to let someone else control the events in life as you follow. Both skills are necessary in order to be successful in life.

Here are some guiding principles to observe when you're a guest at a restaurant for social or business reasons:

- Be on time. If for any reason you are going to be late, call the restaurant so they can pass the information to your host. Try not to cancel the date, but if you do, you must call the host. Don't pass it off to a third party.

- If you arrive before your host, wait patiently until he arrives. If you are seated, don't order anything, and leave your napkin folded.

- If you do arrive late and other guests have already been

served their first course, just pick up from where they are so you won't be out of sync with the others.

- When selecting from the menu, wait for the host to order to see what price range is appropriate. As the guest, you don't want to order the most expensive item on the offering. If, however, the host states that you may order whatever you wish, then you may feel free to order what you like regardless of the cost.

- As the guest, you will sometimes need to sit on your hands. The host is the one who will deal with the waiter—that is his responsibility. If you need something, softly and politely make your request known to your host, who in turn will make it known to the waiter.

- If you're the guest at a business meeting, don't force the introduction of the business topic. Let the host make that decision. Continue your small talk until the host is ready.

- Never arm wrestle to pay the check if you are the guest. It is proper for the host to pay the check (unless otherwise discussed). Be sure to write a thank-you note to the host within three days. Even though e-mail is used in a lot of situations, there is no substitute for a handwritten thank-you note. A follow-up note is appreciated by the host and also signals that you have good manners—that's a good reputation to have.

Manners for Both Host and Guest

- Women should never apply makeup at the table—excuse yourself to the ladies' room to make any adjustments.

- Remember, there are others in the dining room other than yourself. Avoid boisterous levels of conversation.

- Cell phones are not appropriate. If your phone rings, excuse yourself from the table or exit to a convenient place to talk. It's much better to turn your phone off.

- Do not use toothpicks and forks to dislodge food between your teeth. If you can't wait, excuse yourself and go to the appropriate restroom to take out the bothersome food.

- Pace your eating so you don't fall behind those in your party. Keep pace with the others.

- Keep from using your restaurant table as a conference table. If you position letters and written material all over the table-top, the waiter will not have a place to set down your food.

- If you take extra time to finish your meal, consider giving the waiter an extra tip.

- It is impolite to hop from table to table. You cause extra attention to yourself, and it is rude to your host.

- For health reasons, don't use your napkin as a handker-chief—germs can be transmitted to the food handlers who in turn pass it on to other customers. Dismiss yourself from the table if you have a continuous coughing and sneezing spell.

The best index to a person's character is (a) how he treats people who can't do him any good, and (b) how he treats people who can't fight back.

—ABIGAIL VAN BUREN

~ 12 ~

Watch Your Words

Do not let any unwholesome talk come out of your mouths, but only what is helpful for building others up according to their needs, that it may benefit those who listen.

—Ephesians 4:29

We often tell our children to be careful about what they say. However, adults set the tone for the words our children speak. Ask yourself, *Do I walk my talk?* Good language starts at home—Mom and Dad must practice good manners when choosing and using proper words. After all, words are powerful, and they most definitely influence people. Positive words build up, and negative words tear down. Analyze your choice of words and see if your word selections are positive or negative.

Positive Words	Negative Words
I can	I can't
I will	I'll try
I want to	I have to
I'm going to	I should have
My goal	I could have

Today	Someday
Next time	If only
I understand	Yes, but
Opportunity	Problem
Challenging	Difficult
Motivated	Stressed
Interested	Worried
Possible	Impossible
You, your	I, me, my
Love	Hate

Good Words

In the wide world of manners, you would do well to keep in mind a few good words. They will carry you a long way in life from childhood into adulthood. You can never go wrong when you use these words: please, thank you, excuse me, and I'm sorry.

As our culture adopts a sinking standard for what is considered acceptable speech, it is up to us to keep our words positive, uplifting, proper, and kind. These four phrases are a great start and will serve you well.

Bad Words

While watching sitcoms on TV, you'd have to screen out a lot of the dialogue if you eliminated bathroom words. The writers of these scripts seem to always push the limits of civility. But we don't have to give our speech over to bad words. People with good manners don't want to hear and most certainly don't want to use these kinds of words:

Mean comments	Teasing
Back talk	Bathroom talk

Bragging   Rude whispering

Lies   Swear words

Demeaning words

Tone of Voice

Sometimes body language speaks louder than the words you use. Regardless of the words that come out of your mouth, your tone of voice communicates a great deal. When you grumble or mutter, talk down to the ground, make weird noises, or grunt instead of speaking clearly, your words won't matter. All anyone will perceive is the rudeness. Talking like this shows that you don't care about the other person and that you have better things to do. Eye contact goes a long way to signal that you think a person's words are worthy and that you want to hear them. It's respectful, and it's also what you seek from others when you speak.

Compliments

Compliments make other people feel good about themselves. Just make sure you really mean them and are not overdoing it. Be genuine when communicating praise or words of encouragement to another. Compliments should never be given with the expectation that the recipient will then compliment you. Sometimes we want a compliment in return. If we say we like someone's outfit, we tend to wait for them to say the same about our clothing. Release that expectation so you can enjoy the moment of giving someone else a vote of confidence without any need to have it reciprocated. That is real giving.

Not only must we be willing to give compliments, we must know how to receive a compliment. The best thing to do is smile and say, "Thank you!"

If You're Stuck

If you find yourself stuck and aren't sure what to say or do, try to remember the golden rule. Do you like it when people make fun of you? Probably not. Would you like to be told that you're a good person, a good mother, a good father? Sure you would. Ask yourself, *Would I want to hear this to my face?* If you would, go ahead and say it. Watch your words.

Sometimes it's best not to talk at all. Here's a good rule to follow: When you're talking to someone, you should listen at least as much as you talk. You should only be talking half the time. If the person you're talking to is shy, ask him some questions about himself. Avoid questions that can be answered with a simple yes or no. Instead, ask a question that requires some thought and a full answer. Saying, "Tell me what you like about your job" gives someone an opportunity to express himself. People love to talk about their lives. This type of question should get someone talking in no time, and you'll learn a lot about your new friend.

God's road is all uphill, but do not tire,
Rejoice that we may still keep climbing higher.
—ARTHUR GITERMAN

Advice on Making Good Conversation

- Less is better—no need to tell it all.
- Be a good listener. People love to be around sympathetic listeners.
- Good conversation is about give-and-take. Do both.
- Think before you speak.
- Be tactful. You don't need to talk about your most recent surgery.
- Stay light with a good sense of humor.
- Stay away from sarcasm and malice.
- You don't have to be clever, just real.

- Keep away from talking just about you. Me, me, me gets boring.
- Try to find a topic of common ground.
- Silence is acceptable. You don't have to fill in dead air time.
- Be sure to ask other people to share about themselves.
- Don't monopolize all the time with one person. Spread yourself around to others.
- Be polite when you excuse yourself from conversation.

We must learn to be still in the midst of
activity and to be vibrantly alive in repose.

—INDIRA GANDHI

~ 13 ~

The Art of Introductions

When friends are at your hearthside met,
Sweet courtesy has done its most
If you have made each guest forget
That he himself is not the host.

—THOMAS BAILEY ALDRICH

The ability to remember names is really a wonderful gift. Some people have the ability to retain names for years. Others forget the names of acquaintances shortly after meeting them. To be good with names has a lot of advantages. People are always impressed when you call them by name after not seeing them for a while. When being introduced to someone, focus on their name. If a person's name is unusual, I often ask that person to spell it for me—that way I etch the name in my memory. Another good technique for remembering one's name is to write it down on a piece of paper to be referred to at a later date.

Some people don't like name tags, but I find them very helpful at large gatherings. If you have a holiday gathering and invite friends, coworkers, and neighbors, it is very helpful to have the tags. They make it much easier to blend a large group.

Proper Introductions

People in authority (such as mayors, pastors, employers, or parents), older people, or women are spoken to first. The other people are introduced to them. This means you introduce

Did You Know?

Manners are different in different countries and in different groups. In America, it's considered polite to smile at people and to look them in the eye. In some other countries it's considered more polite not to look others in the eye or touch them. In any country, though, kindness and thoughtfulness are always correct—even if you don't know all the rules.

- a man to a woman

- a child to an adult

- a younger person to an adult

- a friend to a pastor

- a citizen to the mayor

To introduce a man to a woman, say, "Christine, I'd like for you to meet Chad Merrihew. Chad, this is Christine Barnes, my granddaughter."

To introduce a child to an older person, say, "Mrs. Whitney, I'd like for you to meet my wonderful grandson Weston Barnes. Weston, I'd like for you to meet Mrs. Whitney—she is one of my neighbors."

When being introduced to someone, ask the person introducing you to repeat the name if you're not sure you heard it properly. If you meet someone you've met before or whom you haven't seen for a long time, help the person by giving your name again: "Hello, I'm Yoli Brogger. We met last year at the fund-raiser for Women of Vision." If someone approaches you in this way, take a cue that the person may not remember your name and reintroduce yourself as well. When you must introduce yourself to someone whose name you have forgotten and hinting doesn't work, confess politely with a smile: "Please help me with your name. I have such an awful memory sometimes." Or, "I'm so sorry. I enjoyed talking with you at Mary's tea last spring, but I've forgotten your name."

When people introduce themselves for the first time, introduce yourself back. For example, at a school's open house another mother may say: "Hello, I'm Barbara, David's mother." That's your cue to say, "It's so nice to meet you. I'm Donna, Anissa's mom. Our children are in the same class."

How to Have a Happy Handshake

- Hold your right hand out with your fingers together and your thumb up.
- Be firm in your grip—not too hard or not too soft.
- Don't make a face if the other person squeezes too hard.
- Don't let your hand go limp. No one wants to shake hands with a jellyfish.
- High-fives and knuckles are only for people you are familiar with. Stick to the traditional handshake in your social settings.
- When a man is introduced to a woman, he should let her offer her hand to shake before he extends his.

~ 14 ~

Handling Social Taboos

Other people see your deeds;
God sees your motives.

—UNKNOWN

Believe it or not, we can and will get into many difficult situations in life. The more exposed we are to the outside world, the more unexpected situations we find ourselves in. Usually there aren't any set rules or literature to help us know how to handle these situations. We'll look at several situations that could be embarrassing and how to handle them with good etiquette.

Yawning. This is where the hand-over-mouth comes into play. If you feel a yawn coming on, the usual clenching your teeth together makes your face look distorted. Simply place your hand over your mouth and very politely say, "Oh, please excuse me, I didn't get a good night's sleep last night."

Rumbling stomach. If you can ignore it, do so. However, if those around you hear it, you might simply say, "It must be near lunch time—at least my stomach thinks so."

Hiccups. These don't rise up too often for most people, but when they do appear they must be dealt with. Medical science says they occur because of stress and tension. (This might give you a clue to examine your lifestyle—you might need to slow down the pace.) Simply excuse yourself for a moment, go to the closest restroom, try some deep breathing, take a drink of water, and repeat if needed. Rejoin who you were talking with and resume your conversation.

Bad breath. Often you are the last person to know if you have bad breath. Make it a point to visit your dentist at least twice a year, brush your teeth after every meal (if possible), and floss on a regular basis. In other words, start out first with good dental health. After that, use breath fresheners before you meet with others. At home have a bunch of parsley in the refrigerator so you can take a clump and chew.

If someone offers you a mint in a crowd, it might be a signal that your breath reflects the garlic you had last evening. Be proactive—take the gesture as kindness and avoid defensiveness.

Sneezing. Sneezes seem to come on in the least desirable situations. However, they do give you a funny feeling in your nose first. They tell you, "Get ready, here I come!" At the first sign of that tingle, try the best you can to have your nose and mouth covered with a napkin, handkerchief, or at least your hand. Turn your head away from the crowd or away from food. After sneezing, just utter, "Please excuse me" in an apologetic tone. Usually those around you will utter back, "God bless."

Accidents at the table. Nothing is more embarrassing than knocking over a glass of water or milk at the table, particularly if you are having a family or business dinner. If accidents do happen at the table, use a napkin to mop up until the waiter arrives to help. If you're at home, you can get some paper towels to absorb the spillage. Simply apologize once to your guests and move on. Handle the situation with as little disruption as possible.

A talker, talker, talker. We have all been trapped by talkers who have never learned to listen. They just go on and on. It's all about them. Often they never come up for air. How do I handle that person? To be honest, I don't want to listen to them all evening.

- Interrupt them occasionally with a question that might divert the conversation.

- Excuse yourself to go to the restroom.

- Excuse yourself so you can go over to a guest that you must speak with.

- Have your spouse rescue you if he or she notes you are being trapped.

- Change the subject often so at least the topic changes.

So you've got a problem? That's good!
Why? Because repeated victories over your
problems are the rungs on your ladder to success.
With each victory you grow in wisdom, stature
and experience. You become a bigger, better, more
successful person each time you meet a problem and
tackle and conquer it with a positive mental attitude.

—CLEMENT STONE

Handling Those
Telephones and Cell Phones

*The Lord has set apart the redeemed
for himself. Therefore he will listen to
me and answer when I call to him.*

—PSALM 4:3 TLB

The increase in cell phone technology has provided great convenience for many of us. However, it seems like wherever we go someone is talking, talking, talking. It has become such a problem that churches, movies, and businesses have posted signs: "Please turn off your cell phones," or "This is a no cell phone area." This tells me that people have abused this new technology and need to sharpen their manners in this area of life. In fact, there is a great need for phone etiquette refreshers for all types of phones and communication.

Basic Phone Etiquette

When to call. Most calls should be placed between eight A.M. and ten P.M. on weekdays, ten A.M. and ten P.M. on Saturdays, and noon and ten P.M. on Sundays. If you are calling out of your time zone area, take into consideration what the difference in time might be. You will need to add or subtract from your standard time zone.

Call waiting. Unless you are expecting a call, let the second call go into the voice mail. If, however, you decide to answer a call, it should be done only to inform caller number two that you will return his call immediately after finishing your present conversation. (Be sure to honor your word and call back immediately.) If you are in the middle of a serious conversation, don't pick up call waiting.

Returning calls. Personal calls should be returned the same day or within a twenty-four hour time span. This is an area where people will determine their thoughts about you as a person. Following up on a timely basis is so important.

Business manners. The receptionist at your office is one of the most valuable assets your company has. This person gives the first impression of who you are or who you aren't as a business and is the first contact and personal interaction a caller has with your company. Good telephone manners are a must. Make sure that the person who represents your company has an upbeat voice, is knowledgeable of the organization's purpose and operation, knows the personnel of the company, and is trained in handling emergencies. A live person is always better than a computerized voice directing phone visitors to "Punch one for customer service, two for new orders, or three for sales." Make sure that if people are put on hold, you come back periodically to update them on the status of the call.

Cell Phone Etiquette

This area of phone etiquette touches on a love-hate relationship. Sometimes a cell phone seems like a difficult family member: You can't live with her and you can't live without her. It gives you a lot of freedom, and that is great. But if you're not responsible, it can become a curse. For some reason, the abuse of the cell phone has become one of America's pet peeves. Many users think the world revolves around their next call. Somehow we have to admit and remember that good cell phone manners need to be exercised while out in public. This is an area where the Golden Rule can be exercised.

Cell Phone Do's

- Use the cell phone for emergencies.

- Answer your cell to connect with family and to conduct business where appropriate.
- Have brief conversations when in public.
- Keep your voice at a low level when around others and out of courtesy for your caller.
- If you have a babysitter waiting at home, be sure to have the phone on at some level.
- When in libraries, restaurants, and other quiet public places, turn your phone off or turn it to vibrate mode.

And Don'ts

- Don't have lengthy conversations when in the presence of others.
- Don't express personal issues, concerns, or worries on a cell phone in public places.
- Don't check text messages or voice mail messages when you are with someone else, unless the call or message will relate to that person as well.
- Don't speak loudly. Cell phones typically have good reception, and you should be able to speak more quietly than normal.
- Don't talk on your phone or your headset device while you are at a customer service counter at stores, banks, or anywhere. It is inconsiderate of the customer service employee, and it holds up the lines.
- Don't use your cell phone conversation as a way to promote your importance or to brag so that others around you can hear your business. Be discreet.

~ 16 ~

How to Support Family Members

He who brings trouble on his family will inherit only wind.

—Proverbs 11:29

We learn how to make new introductions properly, we learn we are to pass our food to the right at a dinner function, and we learn how to place our napkin on our lap, but few of us learn how to support and encourage our family members. Let's explore how we can use good manners with the diverse group we call family. Each family is unique unto itself. Some members are functional and others are dysfunctional—but they are our family. The family should be the most effective support team for each member. Here are some ways to nurture that support:

- Celebrate special occasions such as birthdays, wedding anniversaries, holidays, religious celebrations, and the like.

- Note when something of importance in the family occurs, such as when a brother gets a promotion, a nephew makes the basketball team, a niece plays first chair in the orchestra, or a sister has a new baby. Whatever you do on these occasions, always remember to act—do something. Don't just sit back and say, "Wouldn't it be nice to send a card with a check inside." Do it!

- When a family member is in the hospital…
  - Cheer up that family member with a telephone call at least every other day. Keep the message uplifting, keep it short, and tell them as you close, "I love you."
  - Ask if there is anything you can do for them, such as babysit the children, bring over a meal, or go to the bank.
  - If the phone won't connect to their bedside phone, leave a message with their nurse. She will deliver your message.
  - Take them a collection of family photos to remind them of the people that love them.
  - Recycle the old flowers in the room with new fresh ones.
  - Bring the patient a book or magazine that they might enjoy reading.
- Share with your family the red "you are special" plate for a birthday, an anniversary, a promotion, or good news of any kind—anything to celebrate.
- Present a family member with a gift certificate for four hours of free babysitting.
- Be of assistance when a family member needs to go to a medical visit, check on insurance coverage, or question a medical bill that seems to be in error.
- Take on the responsibility to keep various family members up-to-date on good news or bad news about other members of the family. Be the one who keeps the family informed.
- Be sensitive to various members of the family. They might need help with their finances, their children, their job, their marriage. Offer to help out in any way in which they need help.
- Urge a family member to seek help and counseling if he's facing something bigger than you are skilled to handle.
- Be an encouragement to your nieces and nephews—go to

their schools' open houses, attend their athletic events, attend church performances that they participate in, and write them occasional notes of encouragement.

- Be sure to invite the widow and widower to your family gatherings. We live in a couple's world, and the singles would appreciate being included.

- Plan family get-togethers. Often that may be difficult, since American families seem to be scattered all over the country and frequently in foreign countries. Usually one person in a family will coordinate and make things happen. Choose to be that family member.

- Send greeting cards to relatives to celebrate birthdays, anniversaries, engagements, and weddings and to bring comfort when loved ones are hurt or die.

- Keep a journal of your relatives that you can pass down to other family members. Be the family historian.

It takes a lot of work to keep families together. Children and grandchildren are nurtured to grow up into healthy adults when they sense that they have a knowledge and understanding of those who have gone before them. Heritage is so important in a family structure. Once we are parents, we remain parents regardless of how grown up our children are. We are also always siblings and sons or daughters. We are granddaughters and grandsons. We're always connected to our family, even when we have our own families.

Your success as a family, our success as a society, depends not on what happens in the White House, but on what happens in your house.

—BARBARA BUSH

~ 17 ~

Communication from Afar

He who guards his lips guards his life, but
he who speaks rashly will come to ruin.

—PROVERBS 13:3

We have many options when deciding how to communicate with people near and far. We once were limited to a pen and a piece of paper, but now we live in a new world. Most of us would be lost without our phones, e-mails, fax machines, BlackBerries, Palms, iPods, and so on. Today, the ability to write a good business letter is often overlooked. E-mails are so informal and fast that most of us automatically use them as our primary form of communication.

When communicating with a friend, business associate, or a possible new client for your business, there are a few skills you may want to acquire. After all, becoming a skilled communicator can increase your success, fulfillment, and satisfaction in life. Good etiquette and proper manners come to the forefront when you're trying to have others understand you as a person or as a business.

Below are some tips on how to project yourself and to be a strong and well-mannered communicator. Revisit the cell phone etiquette we discussed earlier and then explore these helpful guidelines for other forms of courteous communication.

Using the telephone. The first impression you give someone on the other end of the telephone is so important. The ability to answer a telephone properly gives either a positive or negative image of who you are.

With personal calls at home, callers automatically get a sense of your mood. If you're cheery, they're glad they called; if downbeat, they can hardly wait to get off the phone. Even though sometimes telemarketers may be on the other end, you can be pleasant and extend a good day to them as you exit the call. In many cases you may be the only cheerful caller they talk to all day. Use these calls to be encouraging to some people today. Remember to bloom wherever you are planted.

Taking calls for a company. You're the first impression that callers have of your company. Your challenge is to transfer calls quickly and cheerfully to the people the callers wish to talk to. Keep your tone of voice bright and cheerful even when times are difficult. If you let the rise and fall of your moods and stresses dictate how you answer the phone, you run the risk of callers being put off by the way you respond to them. They also might think your negative mood is a direct response to them calling! You need to remember to stay calm and positive in your interaction with callers. "Accentuate the positive" is your battle cry.

Answering your own call. If you don't have a receptionist filtering your calls, you may be the one who does your own answering either as a small business owner or as an employee who interacts with the public or other businesses. You might try these initial responses:

- *A greeting:* "Good morning" or "Good afternoon."
- *Name of business:* "This is the A-B-C Company."
- *Name of person speaking:* "This is Christine Merrihew speaking."
- *Direction of action:* "How may I help you?" or "How may I direct your call?"

These greetings present a very professional welcome. If you receive a call when you're in the midst of a stressful situation or you're trying to do three things at once, your voice can still come across as upbeat, calm, and cheerful. Your choice and your attitude will control this important factor.

If you're in the middle of a very important task and don't want to be interrupted, have your calls forwarded to voice mail for a short time. But be sure to respond to your messages as soon as you can and certainly before the end of your workday. Your timely response to messages is very important—your reputation is at stake. If you are lax in returning your calls, you are telling those people that they are not important or their concerns are not worth your time—and that's never a good message.

Even if the caller can't see you, body language is so important when talking on the phone. Yes, the way you sit or stand will affect your tone of voice. If you slump over in your chair, it will affect your breathing. However, if you sit up, your voice will sound positive and energized.

Proper use of voice mail. We've grown accustomed to leaving messages when others are busy, on another line, or away from their desk. It's such a wonderful thing to not miss a person's message just because you are busy or gone. Be sure to keep your outgoing "Thank you for calling" message short and upbeat. This is still a point of first impression for that first-time caller. Make your voice warm and cordial. It's very important that you return the call on a timely basis.

To be most effective, rerecord your voice mail message daily. Record when you will and will not be in the office. In a businesslike voice, ask the callers to leave a brief message and include the time and date of their call. Request them to leave a phone number where they can be reached. Assure the caller that you'll return their calls when you return to the office.

Using text messaging. This has become the new wave of communication, particularly with young members of our society and many professionals. Text messaging is most beneficial when a person does not choose texting over being present for what is happening around them.

Text messaging is nonetheless very much a part of our culture now.

It can be very useful when you need to communicate quick facts or updates to others and you don't have the opportunity for an entire phone conversation. Always keep your messages brief. Keep messages to a few lines, and follow up with a phone call if you need to add more information. Here are a few abbreviations that you can use to shorten messages:

- FWIT: for what it's worth
- IIRC: if I recall correctly
- HTH: happy to help / hope that helps
- TIA: thanks in advance
- FYI: for your information
- BTW: by the way
- OBO: our best offer
- TTYL: talk to you later
- BCNU: be seeing you
- CU2MO: see you tomorrow
- IMHO: in my humble opinion

And there's more. The following visual clues are known as smileys:

- :-)   = smiling
- :-(= frowning
- :-D   = surprised
- :-/   = perplexed

Smileys enable you to communicate how you feel about a subject. They can appear to be flippant, so be really sure that you're sending them in the right context and to a person who is sure to understand and appreciate them.[1]

Using e-mails. Just think, you can send an immediate message from one part of the world to another part of the world and never have to add a postage stamp on the envelope. This form of communication has its good news and its bad news. The good news is that you can quickly send a message to a friend or business associate now. Click on Send, and off it goes. The bad news is that your e-mail inbox can be flooded with all kinds of junk. Many folks complain that they have to sift through tons of entries before they find a meaningful message. Think before you send a mass e-mail to a group of friends. Don't develop a reputation of sending out inappropriate stories and jokes. Use this form of communication for its primary function to send useful material quickly and economically to a friend or business associate.

E-mails are still no substitute for handwritten correspondence. Never use e-mail to invite guests to your home for dinner or for sending a thank-you note to someone who has given you a gift. Nothing can substitute for a graciously handwritten note or letter.

Using the fax machine. Faxes have taken a backseat to e-mails. However, a fax is still sometimes necessary. A fax is not a letter, so you don't have to write "Dear Sheri" or sign off "Sincerely yours." You simply write what you want to convey and sign it personally if you wish.

A fax machine makes unique sounds when it receives a message, so be thoughtful when sending such a message. Reserve faxes for normal business hours, not taking the chance that the fax machine might be in a person's home office—thus waking the recipient in the middle of the night.

In the long run you hit what you aim at.
Therefore, though you should fail immediately,
you had better aim at something high.

—HENRY DAVID THOREAU

~ 18 ~

Parents with Children

The father of godly children has cause for joy.
What a pleasure to have children who are wise.

—Proverbs 23:24 NLT

*H*aving a new child in your home is wonderful for you as parents. It's exciting and important to get out of the confines of your home after being cooped up during the final days of your pregnancy and the first few months of the child's arrival.

Young children are welcome at many occasions and places, but as parents we need to understand that they are not as welcome at many other places. This is a hard lesson to embrace. We get so caught up in our own family unit that all we can think about is what we need. And if we aren't used to thinking through whether situations are child-friendly, we need to make some adjustment and receive new wisdom.

Before you load up the newborn and all the accessories that go with a baby, be certain that the location or social function you are attending is one that is open to children. For example, if you take young children to movies, plays, or intimate restaurants, your child may spoil the events for others.

If you've spent a lot of time and energy preparing for a formal dinner, make sure your guests know whether they should bring their young children. You don't want to be surprised by the arrival of your guest and their small, uninvited child. The other guests would feel uncomfortable or offended if they had made babysitting arrangements for their children.

As a parent you need to evaluate your desires versus the needs of others. You won't be able to attend certain social events out of consideration of others. Watch out for this attitude: "If you can't include my baby, you can't have me!" Unfortunately, that can be a pretty common attitude among parents. Standing up for yourself and your family is good, but be discerning about such blanket statements. Demands like these will only reduce the number of events you'll be invited to, and you'll quickly get a reputation for being thoughtless and selfish.

You can take your children plenty of places that are appropriate, and this phase of your life will be short-lived. Here are certain rules of etiquette to consider when you have young children:

Don't assume that children are automatically invited to private functions. If the invitation doesn't mention children, the omission was probably intentional. If the host wanted to include children, she would have indicated that on the invitation.

Don't call and ask. This will put the host in a bad position. If you are not sure or you don't have someone to care for your children, it is best to not accept the invitation. Missing a function is better than having hurt feelings among friends.

Be thoughtful when visiting friends without children. Not every home will be child friendly. Some have had children who have left the home; others have never had children. When you are making a short visit to chat or to drop something off, be extra sensitive and keep track of your child. You certainly don't want something broken by one of your children. On such an occasion you certainly want to give an advanced alert that you will be dropping by, and always ask if it would be convenient to bring your child.

Consider others as you venture into public. It's up to you to make sure that each of these outings is a learning experience for your child, comfortable for you, and not an imposition on others. The basic etiquette requirement for parents with young children is always consideration for others. Do for others what you hope they would do for you in a similar situation. Here are some specific situations:

Eating out. When you make reservations to a certain restaurant, ask if it is children friendly. Certain eateries are equipped for children, but others aren't. If it isn't, substitute another restaurant. This is a very sensitive area of proper etiquette, but in certain situations, like an anniversary or holiday occasion, you want to consider the clientele of the restaurant. Nothing is worse than taking a young child to a fine restaurant and ruining the other guests' experience. You'll be embarrassed and burdened by the awkwardness, and the meal will be spoiled for everyone. Why put your children in a situation where they won't be wanted or accepted? They may become very uncomfortable and confused. Wait until the children are old enough to handle such an event. This approach is more fair for you, for others, and for the child.

Church functions. Most churches provide wonderful nursery facilities for your children, but if they don't have a setup for childcare, carefully consider the risk of disturbing others during services. If your church has a "cry room," this is great to use when the children are young. If none of the above are provided, please excuse yourself and your children from the service if they start making a fuss or are being quite verbal.

Venues of entertainment. Either indoor or outdoor facilities are not good for young children. The audience is there to be entertained. They didn't buy a ticket to be charmed by your young child. If you have no other alternative, be sure to sit in an area where you can exit if need be.

Whatever the venue, event, or situation, make sure you're sensitive to those sitting near you. Often parents try to calm their babies or young children back into a quiet mode, but those two or three minutes can cause real discomfort for others around your area.

Children are the sum of what parents contribute to their lives.

—RICHARD R. STRAUSS

~ 19 ~

Five Manners Most Parents Forget to Teach

*A child only educated at school
is an uneducated child.*

—George Sanayana

The focus of good manners is not about following rules; it's about bringing order and security to life. Knowing the right things to do gives children and adults confidence, helps to contain emotionally charged situations, and teaches discipline and self-control.

As adults and as parents we can concentrate on teaching five basic areas of manners to our children. You and your children can learn and grow together as you emphasize the following "big five":

1. *Manners at home.* The people we love deserve at least as much courtesy as we offer to strangers. When your children practice good manners with the family on a daily basis, home becomes a place of harmony and peace.

2. *Respect for older people.* Children need to know that older people deserve respect simply because they are older. Showing respect means letting them go first in the grocery line or at a buffet, giving up your seat to them on the bus or train, and most of all, acknowledging their presence graciously.

3. *Awareness of others in public places.* Teach children to respect those around them. They should know such general rules as keeping from talking loudly, holding the door for others, and walking on the right when passing others. At the movies, everyone should know to eat and speak quietly and not to kick the seat in front of him.

4. *Telephone etiquette.* When you place a call, identify yourself, call at an appropriate time, and if you placed a call, be the one to end it. Because so many youngsters have cell phones, we parents should teach the basic etiquette for properly using them.

5. *Conversational courtesies.* Children often aren't aware that a lack of response communicates lack of interest. If someone speaks to you, acknowledge it. Make eye contact when you speak, and learn to listen and to ask questions that draw a person out. This is a vital skill that will benefit children all through adulthood. [1]

Below are a few exercises you can do with your children so you can act out proper manners in a real-life setting:

- Express gratitude both verbally and in notes.
- Hold the door open for any person just behind you as you go through it.
- Men, let women go through the doorway first and open the door for women.
- Demonstrate cell phone etiquette (including being conscientious of when to take calls and voice level).
- Demonstrate courteous phone etiquette: Identify yourself when making calls to familiar people or places.
- Regard others as more important than yourself.
- Properly excuse yourself from one conversation to address

another (instead of disengaging without a word or finishing
the conversation).

- Make good eye contact when listening.
- Demonstrate good table manners.
- Don't exhibit intrusive personal habits (loudly blowing nose,
adjusting trousers, etc.).
- Don't interrupt or talk over someone.[2]

Remember to major on the majors and not on the minors. Concentrate on a few basic manners that will give your children a head
start in life.

*Direct your children onto the right path,
and when they are older, they will not leave it.*
—Proverbs 22:6 NLT

~ 20 ~

How to Eat Various Foods Properly

*The most significant change in a person's
life is a change of attitude. Right
attitudes produce right actions.*

—WILLIAM JOHNSON

Most of us know how to eat basic foods properly, but how does one know how to properly eat certain, in some cases unusual, foods? Below is a brief discussion of some of those different or awkward foods that you'll come across in your at-home and dining-out experiences.

Artichokes. Many people have never experienced this wonderful vegetable. Each leaf is pulled off, dipped into your favorite sauce, and then pulled quietly and delicately through your front teeth. When all the leaves have been eaten, you take a knife or fork to scrape the prickly part off so that the heart may be eaten. Never scrape with your fingers. That's a no-no! Be sure to have an extra plate or bowl provided so your guests can discard the eaten leaves.

Asparagus. If this vegetable is not cooked, you may pick up the stem with your fingers and eat it. However, if it is cooked and soggy or served with a sauce, you would cut it into bite-size pieces and eat it with a fork.

Bagels and lox. This combination is ideal for a finger food. Most

101

delicatessens will present this food item to you with the various components served separately and request that you put them together in an open-face sandwich form. In this case you'll use a knife to spread the cream cheese and a fork to lift the lox and onions into place.

Breads. There's no set rule on how to approach this topic; it all depends on what type of bread you're eating. The normal slice of bread, roll, or muffin may be torn into small bites (2–3 bites at a time). These are buttered and eaten before you tear off another 2–3 bites.

English muffins and bagels may be broken in half and made into half sandwich form. If they're too tough, a knife is permissible to cut into half sizes. The rule is to break the bread if the fiber of the bread is breakable or to cut it if the fiber needs a knife in order to portion it into bite-sized pieces.

Chicken. Southerners, by tradition, usually consider fried chicken a finger food and by heritage will automatically eat with fingers. This can be acceptable on picnics or at beach parties and informal meals. At more formal dinners your poultry will be cooked with wines and sauces, thus eliminating the urge to use your fingers. You'll want to use your knife and fork.

Corn-on-the-cob. This food item is usually served at a very informal meal, so guests may decide between two methods. They can eat the corn holding the cob ends with their hands or with cob skewers, or they can shave the corn off of the cob with a sharp knife and then eat the fruit of their labor with a fork or spoon. If they choose to eat with their hands, they need to take special care to not sound like a pig as they munch the corn with their teeth. Also be aware that a kernel of corn inevitably gets stuck in the spaces between your teeth. Since toothpicks aren't served at the table, excuse yourself politely from the table and go to the restroom to remove the stuck corn.

Desserts. What sweet-tooth guest has ever turned down a refreshing dessert? There are various sizes and shapes of dessert forks and spoons, but most of us don't have these in our flatware inventory. Cakes and pies can be served with a normal fork; custards, ice cream, and crème brûlées need the regular spoon. This way the sides and the bottom of the cup can be scraped clean. We don't want to leave any morsel!

Dips. The rule for dipping chips, crackers, or vegetables is that you only get one dip into the sauce or dressing. No double dipping allowed. Be sure to have an abundant supply of napkins alongside the dip bowl for your guests to wipe their fingers and mouths.

Finger foods. In some social circles, one would be very limited as to what they can eat with their fingers. But generally acceptable finger foods include pretzels, popcorn, potato chips, celery, carrots, candy, crackers, cookies, and cheese snacks. Be sure to wipe your fingers on a napkin after you partake of these food items.

Fish. Be careful when eating fish that the bones don't get into your mouth—and even worse—in your throat. There are two ways to eliminate this from happening: 1) avoid putting bones in your mouth by picking them out of the fish (with a fork) before you put any fish in your mouth, and 2) discreetly remove the fish bones from your mouth with your fingers. Place bones to the side of your dinner plate.

Gravies and sauces. Often we add these to our entrée to give it that special flavor or appearance. They are meant to be eaten along with the meal. If a sauce spoon is not available, it is proper to scoop these with a regular dinner spoon.

Gum. Chewing gum is off limits from the dining room table. Dispose of it before you're seated. Be sure to wrap the gum in paper or tissue before throwing it away in the host's wastebasket.

Olives. These favorites can be served by themselves or mixed with other foods. If they're served separately or on a vegetable tray, they would be considered finger food and may be picked up with your fingers and eaten (it's best to serve those that have no pits). If they appear in a salad, you can pick them out with your salad fork and eat them.

Onion rings. If these delicious offerings are served in a fast-food restaurant, they're finger foods and can be eaten with your fingers. Be sure to use a napkin to wipe your fingers and mouth. If you encounter them in a nice restaurant, they are likely served atop a fine piece of beef. In this case you would cut them into edible sizes and eat them with a fork.

Pizza. This leading fast food is enjoyed by young and old. However, young people with gooey cheeses on their faces look better than older people do. If you lack coordination in getting the pizza from the tray to your mouth, you may want to take a piece, put it on your plate, cut it into small pieces, and use a fork. If you're somewhat coordinated and can risk taking crust, topping, and stringy cheese to your mouth, try the finger food method. Pizza would never be served in a formal setting, so you don't have to worry about that etiquette.

Salads. Vegetables are a vital part of a well-balanced diet. When serving a salad as one of your courses, you have one of two options in how it is prepared and served. If you are tearing the lettuce into small pieces and mixing it with bite-sized vegetables, this salad can be eaten with just a fork. If you're using large pieces of lettuce, be sure to provide a proper knife and fork so your guests can cut the larger pieces into more manageable bite-sized pieces. If you are the guest and no knife is provided, use the side of your fork to cut the lettuce leaves into smaller sizes for easier eating.

Sandwiches. There are many kinds of sandwiches and sandwich-like foods. Some favorites are club, pita, tacos, hot dogs, and sloppy joes. Eat them as finger food, paying close attention to the ketchup, mustard, relish, and hot sauce. Watch that these condiments don't fall out and drip on your new shirt or tie. An abundant amount of paper napkins is required. Sometimes the insides of these spill out over the bread, shell, or bun and fall back to the plate. The tasty morsels that fall to the plate can be eaten by using a fork (often this is the best part of a sandwich).

Shellfish. Legs are pulled off and eaten by hand. Those with claws and bodies can be crushed with a metal nutcracker or pounded with mallets. This meat can be extracted and eaten by removing morsels of delicious meat with sharp little forks provided for such delicacies. Then you may dip the meat into melted butter or sauces. When eating such foods, make sure you don't get so excited that you flip butter or sauces on your clothes or the clothes of the person next to you. If you do, don't hesitate to pay for their cleaning bill.

It's okay to use your fingers when you're served shrimp in its shell. However, if your shrimp has already been peeled, cut it with a knife and use a fork to bring it to your mouth.

Soup. The spoon should be filled with the liquid and drawn away from the bowl before it's redirected to the mouth. To be official, several different spoons can be used when serving or being served soup:

- large oval spoon for clear soups
- large round spoon for cream soups
- small round spoon for broths
- porcelain spoon for Chinese soups
- lacquer soup bowl with Japanese bowl (which may be lifted to the mouth for direct eating of the soup)

Whichever spoon and soup you're eating, you may not slurp. When finished with the soup, you may leave the spoon in the bowl or rest it on the soup plate.

Spaghetti. Against common thought, pasta is not to be twirled against a spoon—not even in Italy. It is twirled on the fork against the plate until it makes a tight ball so that it can be raised to your mouth. Make sure the sauce doesn't drip on your clothes. It's proper to ask for a bib if you want to be extra careful.

Steak. Provide the proper steak knife so you don't have to wrestle with the piece of meat to cut small edible bites.

Sushi and sashimi. On the West Coast you will find almost as many sushi bars as you will Starbucks coffee cafés. Every block and every strip mall seems to have at least one restaurant that specializes in sushi. Sushi is lifted clear from the serving plate with chopsticks, dipped into the soy sauce with green horseradish mixed in, and then lifted to the mouth. It is usually eaten in one huge bite. Sashimi must be eaten with chopsticks or a fork.

Tomatoes. These are so messy that if you aren't careful, the juice can get all over your outfit and leave stains. Put a whole cherry tomato in your mouth and clamp down on it with lips firmly closed. Make sure nothing squirts out of the corner of your mouth. If you need to cut up your larger tomatoes into more manageable bite-sized pieces, cut with the side of your fork and then eat the smaller pieces.

Vegetables. Cooked vegetables seem to slip around the plate when you try to catch them with a fork. Raw vegetables are so crisp that you're afraid everyone can hear you chew. It's okay to use a piece of bread or a knife blade as a pusher, and be sensitive that fresh vegetables can make a lot of noise. You're usually not as loud as you think.

Yogurt. One would never eat yogurt from a cup at a formal breakfast, lunch, or dinner. If you are to serve yogurt at your meal, place it in a serving bowl, put your fruit on top of the yogurt, and serve with a spoon.

When you're through changing, you're through.

—BRUCE BARTON

~ 21 ~

The Art of Meeting People

Old friends are always best, unless you can find a new one to make an old one out of.

—Unknown

Good manners don't let us treat one person well and another person poorly just because of their differing social status. The mail carrier is extended the same kindness as the bank president. Our relationships with everyone are important. Someone might ask you, "Don't you get tired of being nice to everyone?" If you're doing it with the right motive, the answer would be no. If, however, you go back and forth in your attitude and treatment of others depending on who the person is, the answer would be yes. Mark Twain once said, "Always tell the truth. That way you can always remember what you tell others."

If good manners are a habit, you don't have to wonder whether you are treating someone properly because you treat everyone alike. With good manners, attitude is as important as the act. The ultimate success of anything you do depends on how nicely you do it. Always keep the Golden Rule on the front of your brain. Check periodically to see if your walk is the same as your talk.

If you find a successful person, you will find many friends who have helped him along the way. Very few of us are self-made. Friends are an absolutely necessary ingredient in the recipe of our own success in life. Good friends make it all worthwhile.

Every person that we meet has the potential to become one of our good friends. Try not to make snap judgments about people when you first meet them. Your first thought may be that they are not too exciting, but you can always be surprised after they become some of your favorite people.

In order for you to have good friends, first you must meet them, and second, you must be a friend to have friends. You must be a person who enjoys meeting others yourself. Here are some ways you can get off to a good start:

- Walk around with a cheery face. A smile always draws attention to your demeanor in life. Look like you would be a good friend. No one wants a grouchy friend—a bad attitude drives people away.

- When at a gathering, look like you're having fun. Introduce yourself to people you've never met. Light changes a dark room into a cheery setting. You be that light.

- Don't be a victim even if you feel miserable. No complaints with hurting feet or sniveling about a hard day at work. Radiate an upbeat temperament. If you've got complaints and problems, see a psychologist or pastor. Don't expect others at a party to solve your disappointments in life.

- Treat every person as a "wow" experience. You might be surprised to find out that that a seemingly boring person has the potential to be a future friend.

- You will meet people only by getting out of your rut and routine. Get out of that house, away from your repetitious lifestyle, and into a new routine.

- Take a self-appraisal and identify what your passion and interests are in life. Then begin to branch out and meet with like-minded people.

- Don't turn down an invitation to a party. You never know, maybe that's where that new friend will be.

- Blind dates may be scary for you, but who knows? That blind date may include some exciting friends you would enjoy meeting—it wouldn't be the first time.

- Be open to joining new clubs that specialize in your interest, such as ski clubs, book clubs, hiking associations, or a theater group.

- Churches and nonprofit organizations are always looking for volunteers. This type of meeting place can be very uplifting because you are giving of yourself and not always getting from others.

- Becoming a hospital volunteer is another way to give of yourself. The contacts also open up a new avenue for new friends.

- Cultural activities are a great place to be involved either as a season ticket holder or just a one-performance ticket buyer. Chance things happen at the intermission—you get to meet others, conversations start, and business cards are exchanged.

- Start associating with like-minded people at sporting events you enjoy. Improve your tennis, golf, or snow skiing skills to the point where others would invite you to be a partner. Others will see your skills and want to play with you. From there you may be invited to a bite to eat.

- Helping out at your child's school is always a great way to meet other people who may be volunteering there as parents as well.

- Whatever you do, keep your eyes open. Pay attention to those people who live in your neighborhood.

Make an Acquaintance a Real Friend

- One of the best ways to make new friends is to invite some guests to a meal. You might prepare it yourself, invite them to a breakfast, or schedule a luncheon appointment. If that goes well, try a more formal dinner engagement.

- If you think your new friend would feel more comfortable with others around, invite a few other people or couples to join you in that first outing.

- You need not always expect to be on the receiving end of invitations. It's important that you learn to be a giver too. Your invitation doesn't always have to be like theirs. Instead of another meal, you might invite them to go to a sporting event, a play, or a gathering to feed the poor.

- Good friends protect their friends from gossip and criticism from others. Be willing to come to the defense of a friend if need be.

- Good friends stay in touch, even when they are busy. Often you have to be flexible to fit in activities that might not be convenient. Be willing to accommodate your friend's schedule.

- The best friends are your 2:00 a.m. friends. They, as well as you, are always available in an emergency. Be willing to babysit at the last minute, pick up your friends' children from school, run an errand when needed, or help them move on the weekend. Be willing to do the unexpected.

- When you feel that your friends are having difficulty with their emotions, be willing to give them some slack. Be ready to help if you need to.

What Good Friends Do

- Avoid overstepping your bounds just because you're a good friend.

- Make compromises for the friendship. Things don't always have to go your way.

- Plan surprises for a friend like a birthday party, a secret gift, an impromptu movie, or a quick cup of coffee.

- Handle drop-by visits graciously. Don't worry that your home isn't perfectly clean. Greet a friend cheerfully!

- Give a small gift for no reason except for the pleasure of seeing the joy on a friend's face.

- Fill in at the last minute to help with a carpool, loan someone a vacation home for the weekend, or help to plan a birthday party for someone else's young daughter.

What makes good friends so special? Sometimes the simplest answer is the most profound: You like them. You feel better when they're around. You enjoy their company. Their presence refreshes you.

Some friendships are as comforting and comfortable as a well-worn pair of shoes. Others are full of excitement and adventure. The best ones are filled with laughter and softened with tears and strengthened with a spiritual bond. And here's something else about a friend: You share something in common. It might be a history, a life circumstance, a set of beliefs, or a certain commitment to a cause. Whatever it is, when you're with a friend, something feels familiar and good.

Your friends sharpen you. They soften you. You want to become the person that a friend sees in you. What do my friends see in me?

Kindred spirits are not so scarce as I used to think. It's splendid to find out there are so many of them in the world.

—Lucy Maud Montgomery, *Anne of Green Gables*

Minor Social Annoyances

*Wearing a lobster bib doesn't strip
a man of his masculinity.*

—UNKNOWN

We all need a little help knowing how to handle some minor social annoyances. Do we, or don't we? That is the question. Guests just show up, and we aren't sure how to handle them. Here are a few tips:

To hug or not to hug. If the person is a close friend or relative, it's perfectly okay to give him a hug. Remember not to squeeze the air out of his body, particularly if you're bigger than he is. However, if you are being introduced for the first time, hold off on the hug but extend a hand for a shake and a "Hello, I'm glad to meet you!"

Sorry, what's your name? You may have a "senior moment" and be unable to recall a person's name (that's why I like name tags). It's quite proper to say, "I'm sorry, but could you refresh my memory? I've forgotten your name." Don't try to fake it—that will just make things worse. On occasion, someone might call you by the wrong name. If it bothers you, you can very politely give him your correct name. If it doesn't bother you, just carry on and ignore the error.

Let's have lunch together. Don't say it if you don't mean it. Often one is tempted to make such a comment to be cordial. If you aren't sincere don't suggest it. If you do mean it, be sure to follow up in a few days to put such a lunch on the calendar.

Watch your language. Be sensitive to those around you. Don't be disrespectful to those in your presence by using improper language. Off-color jokes and the use of four-letter words are never appropriate. Be very respectful at all times. This also is a sign of self-respect.

Being late. This is a bad habit that seems difficult for some people to get a handle on. Tardiness shows disrespect for the people waiting. One doesn't want to have a reputation of being late. It's rude to call someone at the time you're supposed to meet them to tell them you will be late. This gives them no time to adjust their plans, and they are left to wait or are forced to decide to cancel because of your lack of planning. Sometimes you will be late, and that can be excusable occasionally—emergencies do occur. Just don't make it a habit.

Yelling, whispering, and gossiping. What would a ball game be without yelling? Or a good movie without whispering to a friend? But gossiping is never appropriate. Your friends will honor and respect you when they know that you can honor private and confidential information. Great friendships don't permit gossiping. Protect your own reputation by protecting that of others.

No nail clipping in public. Even though one may be bored or has time to kill, don't clip your fingernails or toenails in public, and don't polish them either. If these areas need maintenance, either visit a nail salon or take care of them at home, but never in public. A big etiquette error is to polish your nails in confined spaces like small rooms or airplanes. The fumes can cause headaches, and taking care of personal hygiene in public places is never appropriate.

Consider the volume of your music. Never can I recall a time when music was so much a part of the culture. If you are someone who enjoys listening to music while you are at home or at work or enjoying time at the beach, remember to keep the volume at a personal listening level. The person next to you may not like your choice of music (I know that's hard to believe). The person in the cubicle next to you gets distracted from his work because of your music selection. If playing music is frowned upon during the day, then save your tunes for after-work hours at home (still be considerate of your neighbors).

Chewing gum. Nothing is refreshing like a fresh stick of gum. It curbs your appetite, softens a dry mouth, and gives you something to do when you're bored. However, some rules apply when you decide to stick that gum in your mouth. If you are with others, make sure you offer them a stick too. When in public, please don't smack your jaws, blow bubbles, or snap your gum while chewing. You will find plenty of gum-free zones and scenarios, including offices, job interviews, church, a baby dedication, or a romantic evening.

Breakfast guests. There will be occasions when you have overnight guests who will be eating at your breakfast table. People are more selective about what they eat at breakfast than at any other meal of the day. We all get set on what we like for breakfast. Extend your courtesy by asking your overnight guests what they would like for the wake-me-up meal. They will be grateful if you can accommodate them.

Going Dutch treat. It's quite proper to go out for a meal and pre-arrange to go Dutch treat, meaning each person pays his own way. Often a waiter will provide you with separate bills. Decide upon this arrangement beforehand so there is no misunderstanding when it comes time to pay the bill. However, if you ask someone out to dinner, it is generally understood that the one who does the inviting will pay. The invitee will be your guest.

On lending and borrowing items. Always remember that what's yours is yours. If an item hasn't been returned in an appropriate time period, it is perfectly proper to ask the borrower if you could have it back.

Receiving the wrong gift. We have all received clothing that is the wrong size, out of style, or the wrong color. Perhaps someone has given you a décor item that doesn't fit your home. What do you say or do to not offend the givers? Depending upon your relationship with them, you may be very sensitive in how you approach the subject. Usually honesty is the best manner. First, thank them for their thoughtfulness by giving you the gift and second, explain to them your dilemma and share what you would like to do to correct the situation. In most cases, they will understand and agree with what you would like to do.

Asking for money. One should not openly ask for money as a gift. However, if you receive money, you can be most appreciative for the gift. Gifts should be freely given, not asked for. Be grateful for any gift you receive. As a grandparent, I often give money when I'm not sure of what my grandchild might like as a gift. With the gap between the generations, I'm not always up on the latest fashions and high-tech gadgets. And when you give children money, they have a chance to learn how to manage it.

Exchanging gifts with friends of means. Gift giving is not a contest of who can give the most expensive gift. You're only able to give what you can give. Your friendship is not based on money, so don't be in competition when it comes to gift giving.

Charges that have an error. Being a good consumer requires that you check your bill when you are at the market, restaurant, or store. We are all capable of making wrong additions. Don't take for granted that the bill is correct. If you find you've been overcharged (or undercharged, for which you deserve an A-plus for being honest), quietly speak to the person responsible for your bill. If there's an error, it will be corrected, and it becomes a learning experience for you and the store.

*Making others feel good
makes you feel good!*

~ 23 ~

Business Has Its Etiquette Too

*The wise are glad to be instructed, but
babbling fools fall flat on their faces.*

—PROVERBS 10:8 NLT

On TV, in newspapers, and in magazines, we see where a CEO of a large company falls from grace. Business leaders were once thought of so highly, yet now they're looked upon in an unfavorable light. How did this fall from grace take place? A shift in values taught at home is part of the issue. Once parents were teaching their children certain ethical values, but now we see that many children aren't being taught at a young age how to be fair in dealing with others. The morals that adults instill in their children by talking to them and acting as mentors impact the way young people lead their public and private lives.

Our behavior defines how people judge us. Manners make society function and motivate people to work with one another. When good etiquette and manners are evident in an organization, they spread over to the consumer. A well-mannered company has a very positive effect on those who are on the outside looking in. From the loading dock personnel to the receptionist who greets you, you get a sense that this is a company you want to do business with.

These people skills are really just good old-fashioned manners. Good manners are built into the structure of our character, and they can't be turned on or off depending on how you feel or depending on what time of day it is.

Good Business Behavior

Good manners are good for business. Common sense (which isn't so common anymore) and consideration for others win respect and identify you as a team member who is a real asset to your company. Good business manners start at the top and flow down throughout the organization.

- Be consistent in how you treat people. The low man on the totem pole should be treated with the same respect you would extend to your boss. Remember to be nice to all people as you advance up the ladder, and you will help build a better company.

- Exhibit loyalty to your boss both inside as well as outside the business. Don't say anything about someone that you wouldn't say to them directly.

- Hold off criticizing another coworker unless you are his supervisor, and then do so only when face-to-face and in private.

- Be helpful to the new kid on the block. The first few days have a lot of unknowns. Be willing to show new people around—introduce them to others in the department. Give them heads-up information about office procedures. Treat them with the Golden Rule in mind.

- Be known as a person who stands by his word. If you pledge that you're going to do something, do it.

- Be punctual with appointments and meetings. Don't be known as one who is always late for meetings.

- Develop a sense of humor. Humor sets the tone for a more casual and relaxed atmosphere. People like to be around people who can laugh.

- Don't be known around the office as a taker. If a lunch is paid by someone else, the next time you can pay the bill. Be known as someone who can pick up a check.

- Be nice to everyone. After all, they will play a big part of you getting a promotion within the company. Learn early in life that the clerical staff and receptionist are as key to your success as your managers.

- Don't overexaggerate how important you were in your last job. Be humble about your importance. Others in the office will be attracted to someone who downplays his importance.

- Don't ever put someone down—not in public or in private.

- Be willing to share the credit for a job well done. Don't try to collect praise for something not really of your doing.

- Get in the habit of saying "we" did this or did that. Get out of the habit of saying "I" did this or that. It helps develop team spirit.

- If you are willing to take credit, you also have to be willing to take the blame for something that went wrong.

- Return telephone calls and e-mails on a timely basis—at least within 24 hours.

- Respond to important written correspondence as soon as possible—within five working days.

- Respond within a week after receiving an invitation to an event. Be sure to attend if you have accepted the invite. Respond to all RSVPs.

- Don't borrow something from someone in the office if you aren't planning to return it. Make sure it's in good condition when you return it.

- If someone is hospitable to you, make sure you return the favor to them. A thoughtful thank-you note is always appreciated when someone does a favor for you or is helpful in some way.

- Dress appropriately for the office and for any social event pertaining to an office function. Make the company executives and employees proud that you are representing them.

- Be willing to show sorrow when a fellow worker has received bad news.

- Share common information with your fellow workers. No one likes to be left out of the loop.

- Don't steal from your company. That includes stamps, pencils, computer time to do personal business, and lengthy telephone time to handle personal agendas. Remember, time is worth money.

- Talk respectfully about your spouse and children.

- People who are gracious with their notes are appreciated. A person who writes personal notes is remembered fondly and gets ahead in life.

- Use your words to build people up and not to tear them down. Be known as an encourager.

- Remember to thank the people who work hard to make your job possible. Even be willing to add a personal thank-you to their personnel file.

Added Etiquette for the Boss and the Employee

- Have good telephone manners:
  - It's okay to place your own phone calls.
  - Be considerate of other people's time and don't keep them on hold for too long.

- If you receive a call during an appointment, tell the caller that you will call him back as soon as you are finished.

- Remember that everyone is very busy, so when you talk on the phone, be sure to get to the point. Respect the other person's time commitments.

- Occasionally you will dial the wrong number. When you do, apologize to the other person.

• Rise and stand when another person enters your office. Be respectful and stand away from your desk.

• Know how to introduce people properly—a younger person to a more senior one, a nonofficial person to a person with a title.

• Use a firm handshake when you are introduced to a person or when you tell a person goodbye.

• Practice how to make small talk with people. The art of good communication is important to practice at a business function. Many times a company will value a person with good social skills over a more talented or educated person. It's important to learn how to talk about unimportant things.

• When traveling with a superior, give him the best seat in a restaurant, taxi, or limo.

• Take care of all luggage matters (unless told otherwise), tipping, checking into hotels, ordering rental cars, paying the bills for meals, transportation. Depending upon the size of the company, these particulars may be already prearranged.

• Remain silent when your boss is looking over business papers while on a plane, train, limo, or bus.

• Make it a top priority to assist your boss in any way you can.

• Being an assistant to your boss is a great opportunity to

watch and learn while on the job. Many of today's CEOs started out as assistants. It is a great networking opportunity. You meet all kinds of important people.

There's only a slight difference between keeping your chin up and sticking your neck out, but it's a difference worth knowing.

—UNKNOWN

The Art of Helping

We make a living by what we get, but
we make a life by what we give.

—WINSTON CHURCHILL

It's always difficult when you hear about a friend or relative who has an illness, a death, or a terminal diagnosis. What am I to do? What do I say? What should I say? We all want to be sensitive during this time of need. How can I help?

Just do it! Often one says, "Call me if you would like a meal, a pot of soup, or an errand run." But it is more helpful to just do it for the person. Don't wait to be called. If you say you are going to pray for that situation, jot a note in your prayer notebook and be sure to follow through with your promise.

Be sensitive to time. Don't overstay your welcome. Make your visit sweet and brief. Be very sensitive to the energy level of the one you are visiting. It's better to stay too briefly than too long. Leave before the person wants you to leave. Remember, you may not be the only telephone call or the only visit for the day.

Don't ask for too many details. Don't make a patient or caregiver have to tell the same story over and over again. You are not the only person he has had to tell. Just be satisfied with the speedy report. You don't have to know everything.

Guard the articles, videos, DVDs, and cassette tapes you send. We know you are well-meaning when you send all those miracle products, but in most cases they bring confusion and doubt to the patient or family member. One of the important parts of recovery is that the patient has utmost confidence in the medical provider. Yes, it's true that we need the latest information in order to make wise decisions, but the patient doesn't have the time or energy to research all the marketing products on the subject. All these product suggestions are overwhelming to patients and cause them to doubt their doctors. The patient needs encouragement, not more alternatives.

Send a note. Here are some samples of what you might write:

- We send you greetings of love and wishes of comfort. May you find comfort in each other's arms as you wage this most valiant battle. You are in our thoughts and in our prayers, this day and always. The future must seem frightening. I'll stay close. How I wish I could make this cup pass from you. I'd like to take a magic wand and make it all go away. Since I can't do that, please know that I love you and will be with you as you travel this road through uncharted territory.

- I pray for you every morning when I take my walk [or any other specific time you pray for your friend]. I have been praying specifically for _____.

- May you feel supported and loved by the knowledge that we care and are praying for you. I have no idea what the future holds for any of us, but I know who holds the future. May you experience a gentle calmness during this storm in your life. In whatever lies ahead, may you feel God's gentle touch and know He is with you.[1]

Pray. Here is a model prayer you can use:

Lord, I come before You with _____. I thank You that You are the great physician. You made our bodies and know precisely how they function. Lord, it is my desire that You totally and completely heal _____'s body of this illness. Thank You, Lord, that You love _____ and have a future and a hope for him that cannot fade away. You promise to carry _____ through no matter what is ahead, and You promise never to leave him. Give him the peace and assurance of Your constant presence. I ask all these things according to Your will, knowing that Your ways are high above our ways and that Your grace is sufficient. Amen.[2]

Take along a gift. Here are some suggestions:

- bubble bath, body lotions, bath gels
- flowers
- a basket of foods
- an inspirational book
- soothing CDs
- a stuffed animal
- a tea in a basket, including cup, saucer, and scones
- healthy foods to snack on: granola bars, fruit juices, nuts, and a little bit of sweets
- stationery and postage stamps
- for a male, bring a sports magazine, toiletries, a razor, shaving cream
- donate blood in the name of the patient
- a basket from Bath and Body Works
- a fresh new nightie
- Write out some promises from Scripture that would be an encouragement to the reader. Here are some to choose from:
  - Jeremiah 29:11
  - Psalm 27:14

- – Isaiah 43:5
- – Psalm 30:5b
- – Psalm 28:6
- – Psalm 23:1-6
- – Psalm 18:2
- a daily newspaper
- a gift certificate for three hours of work around the house
- a favorite DVD

A cheerful giver does not count the cost of what he gives. His heart is set on pleasing and cheering him to whom the gift is given.

—JULIAN OF NORWICH

~ 25 ~

The Etiquette of Caring

*I define love thus: The will to extend
one's self for the purpose of nurturing one's
own or another's spiritual growth.*

—M. Scott Peck

Pat answers or even words of wisdom or comfort can never remove the pain from a friend's life, but you can make a difference in the lives of those who hurt and are in pain. They need your compassion, love, and support. The following do's and don'ts can help you as you help your friends.

Do's and Don'ts

Do respond in a timely manner with a card, a call, or a visit.

Don't wait a long time before you make your initial contact.

One of the hardest parts of reaching out is the first contact. We are nervous about what we'll say and how we'll be received. We feel sad, burdened, and scared with the news, so we're not sure we have anything to offer. Prayerfully ask God's guidance for what you will say or what you will write in a card. Then, step out in faith and write, call, or visit your hurting friend. Once you've made the initial contact, you'll find follow-up calls are much easier.

Do offer simple, understanding statements, such as these:

> "I feel for you during this difficult time."
>
> "This must be very hard for you."
>
> "I share your feelings of loss."
>
> "I wish I could take the hurt away."

Comments like these let people know you acknowledge their pain and that it's okay for them to feel that way.

Don't try to minimize their pain with comments like these:

> "It's probably for the best."
>
> "Things could be worse."
>
> "You're strong. You'll get over it soon."
>
> "You know God is in control."

Comments like these might be an attempt to offer hope, but to a hurting person, they sound as though you don't comprehend the enormity of what happened.

The first thing we need to do is acknowledge that a crisis or loss has happened. Our comments will then validate hurting persons' feelings. When we minimize or trivialize their feelings, we show that we don't understand the depths of their feelings or that we are not interested in how they feel.

Do be available and be specific with what you want to do to help.

Don't offer vague questions or statements, such as "Is there anything I can do to help?" or "If there is anything you need, give me a call."

Go to them. Your presence is far more important than your words. Be aggressive with your willingness to help. Ask yourself, *What would I need if I were in a similar situation?* Offer specific things you can do for them, such as these:

"I'm on my way to the store. What can I pick up for you? Do you have any milk?"

"Would tomorrow be a good day to help you with the laundry?"

"Would the children like to come over and play this afternoon?"

Don't leave the ball in their court. Most of the time, people in a crisis can't decide or don't know what they do need and would never dream of asking because they do not want to impose.

Do expect that they will be different once they have experienced a tragedy.

Don't make statements like these:

"When will you be your old self again?"

"You need to get over this."

"Just put this behind you."

"You're not the same."

Once people's lives have been touched by tragedy, they will never be the same. They will never be their "old self" again. They will find a "new normal" and ultimately discover a way to go on with life, but it will never be the same again. Our lives have continued despite what has happened in their lives, and for that reason we tend to want life to go back to the way it was before their crisis. Remember the faces of the victims' families at the memorial services one year after 9/11? It was evident they have not "gotten over it." President Bush offered comfort and condolences while the families held up photographs of their loved ones. Tears streamed down their faces; they sobbed at their losses and collapsed into each other's arms for solace and support. Your friends, facing their own crises, tragedy, and loss feel no less pain than those families.

Do agree when the individual expresses his feelings with statements like these:

> "That doesn't make sense."
>
> "It isn't fair."
>
> "I don't understand why this happened."

Don't offer spiritual answers or explanations. We don't know why tragedies happen or why certain people go through trauma.

We do our friends a disservice by offering possible explanations. We have no idea why a tragedy happened. Tragedy isn't fair, and it doesn't make any sense. During a time of crisis, people are apt to question their faith. Why has such a thing happened? Where was God when it happened? They don't need to hear horror or success stories of people you know who've been through something similar. Telling someone that everything will be all right when you have never known the depth of his hardship is an empty statement.

Do give spiritual encouragement from your heart and include Bible verses that have comforted you at a difficult time.

Don't quote Bible verses as a way to correct or minimize their feelings. Never offer spiritual suggestions from a position of superiority or self-righteousness.

Put yourself in the other person's place. Empathetic responses are healing to those going through a difficult time. Think very carefully before using any Scripture. Ask yourself if a passage will communicate comfort or condemnation. "All things work together for good" is never a quote for people in pain. If they claim that verse themselves, then you can affirm that promise, but never offer it as a comfort. At this moment, nothing feels good to them.

Do encourage them to keep a journal or share their feelings with you.

Don't say, "You shouldn't feel that way."

Often just seeing their thoughts on paper helps them deal with what they are facing. Encouraging a free flow of feelings will help them know you care and are not afraid of their pain. Feelings are not right or wrong. Feelings just are. We need to validate them where they are.

Do offer specific statements and questions like these:

> "I have been praying for you."
>
> "Has this week been any better?"
>
> "Is there something especially difficult you are facing?"

Don't open the wrong door by asking, "How are you?"

The real answer to the question "How are you?" is usually something like awful, terrible, or devastated. Your hurting friend won't really want to verbalize that. The best thing to do is to greet your friend with a simple, "Hi, _____," and make a statement of your support or ask a specific question.

Do listen to their hearts.

Don't fill silence with meaningless phrases ("I know just how you feel") or your own stories ("A friend of mine...").

Listening is a powerful tool—don't underestimate its value. Listen with attentiveness. Allow the conversation to flow wherever it needs to go. Don't be afraid of silence. Your presence is the important part. Ask how they are feeling: "What are you struggling with right now?"

You can't possibly know just how they feel. Even if you have faced a similar experience, share only how you felt; don't presume to know how they feel. Your hurting friends do not want to hear about someone else's similar experience.

Do tell them you are praying for them. Ask for specific requests.

Don't make light of prayer with clichés like these:

> "Don't worry, God is with you."
>
> "Everything will be okay."
>
> "Just have faith."

Don't say, "I'm praying for you" in a lighthearted attempt to make them feel better. Make sure to spend time before the Lord in prayer, bringing petitions of need. Ask for specific prayer requests, such as getting a good night's sleep, playtime for their children, or peace in upcoming decisions.

Do say, "I'm so sorry." Then you can add helpful comments like these:

- "This must be so difficult."
- "I know how special he was to you."
- "I share your loss."
- "I want to help…"
- "I've been praying for you."

Don't say, "I'm sorry," and end the sentence. Your hurting friends are sorry too, but they can't respond to "I'm sorry." Add a comment or thought that they can respond to.

Following my statement, "I'm so sorry," I often add, "Was this sudden?" or "Had she been ill?" or "Were you able to be there?" Saying "I'm sorry" is one of the most important things we can say, but it doesn't provide a lead-in for a response. Think ahead. What could you say or ask that will allow your hurting friends to respond to your comment?

Do allow them all the time they need to deal effectively with the phases of their crisis.

Don't put timetables on your hurting friends' recovery.

Your inference that they are not coping well hinders their progress. There are no timelines for recovery, healing, or restoration following a crisis. Don't compare their experience with someone else in a similar situation. Each person handles his or her difficult times differently.

Do offer support and encouragement. Respond cautiously and prayerfully with uplifting and edifying ideas when your friends ask for guidance.

Don't offer advice. If it wasn't solicited, your suggestions may not be appreciated.

Advice is not the same as comfort. Our hurting friends need our nonjudgmental interactions. They need us to offer unconditional love, encouragement, and support. Never give advice unless you have been specifically asked, and even then, be very cautious. We want only to be helpful, but often our advice is not wanted.

When you are asked questions or for advice, share only what you have experienced in your own life. Don't tell stories you have heard about others in a similar situation. Don't say, "I think you should" or "I don't think you should." Until they are much further down their path of recovery, they really aren't looking for input, answers, or solutions.

Do remember especially hard times.

Don't forget anniversaries, birthdays, death dates, and holidays.

Your life may have returned to normal, but your friends live with their crises on a daily basis. Nothing is normal about their lives. Show your continued support by remembering difficult days. Send a card, make a call, or invite them to spend time with you.

Do use your gifts and talents to help. Consider what you enjoy doing and what you're good at.

Don't put yourself under pressure to perform tasks that you really don't want to do.

Use your skills and talents, and function within your gifts to reach out to others in need. If you are not a good cook, don't feel you must bring a meal. Think of ways you can help that are unique to you.

Do understand that each person's experience is unique. Needs, hurts, and emotions will vary from person to person, situation to situation.

Don't say, "I know just how you feel" or "I understand what it's like."

Be honest about your experiences. If you haven't endured their particular kind of tragedy, say, "I haven't been through what you're facing, but I want you to know I care about you and will support you through the difficult time ahead." If you have had a similar crisis, tell them about it briefly, adding that you can empathize with their feelings. Of course you can't completely understand what it is like for them because you haven't been through the past experiences that have laid the foundation for their reaction.

Do continue to keep in touch, offering support, letting them know you're praying for them. Send thoughtful notes with encouraging words.

Don't ignore their needs after the immediate crisis has subsided.

Stay in touch. After a crisis, our lives go back to normal, but the lives of our hurting friends will never be the same.

Do realize that their hearts are full of pain and turmoil. Let them know that you will listen to their feelings and that you want to be a part of the healing process.

Don't expect optimism or levity or happiness from your hurting friends.

Your hurting friends have a shroud of heartache around their hearts, so it is very difficult for them to feel any joy. They often will feel guilty for laughing or having a good time or will resent other people enjoying themselves.

Do indicate your love by saying, "There is nothing that I can say to undo what has happened, but I want you to know that I love you. I'm praying for you, and I want to help."

Don't offer clichés or trite statements in an attempt to minimize what they're facing or to cover up your own insecurities.

Try to imagine what your life would be like if you were facing the same difficulty. Pray with them, show you care, and hurt with them.

Do allow your hurting friends to make the decisions and take the necessary steps to deal with the trauma. No one can tell another what to feel or not to feel.

Don't use statements such as *should* or *if only*. Avoid comments like these:

> "You should go back to work and get over this."
>
> "You shouldn't feel that way."
>
> "If only you'd spent more time with him."
>
> "If only you'd seen it coming."

We minimize people's feelings when we tell them they should or shouldn't feel that way. Their reality is that they *do* feel that way. They are sharing their concerns, fears, and burdens. Catch yourself anytime you hear the words *should* or *shouldn't* formulate in your mind. Most hurting people have already beaten themselves up with thoughts like these:

> You should have more faith.
>
> If only you had been there for him.
>
> If only you hadn't been so strict.
>
> If only you ate better.

Do provide long-term, unconditional support. Let them know that everyone deals with trauma in a different way.

Don't be critical or judgmental. Don't make unhelpful comments like these:

> "This wouldn't have happened if…"
>
> "There must be sin in your life."
>
> "You're not trusting God with this."
>
> "You reap what you sow."

There is no manual or timetable for how to handle a crisis. Let your hurting friends know that you have no expectation of how much time it should take or how they should behave. Assure them that whatever it takes, you will be there with them.[1]

A True Story

When an Air Force chaplain of 30 years was asked about the most valuable lesson he learned about comforting, he relayed this story:

> The most valuable lesson I learned happened just a few months after I had been ordained. I was in my twenties and assigned to Amarillo Air Force Base in Texas. Outside the base was a ramshackle community where the residents lived in old World War II temporary housing. A couple worked as caretakers. The husband was a handyman, and his wife looked after the area.
>
> One night another chaplain called me. "Get the police! There's been a murder in Cammes Village." I'd never handled a murder before, and I drove out to the village not knowing what I'd do or say.
>
> When I arrived, I found that the son of this couple had brutally murdered his fiancée. Too stunned to do anything significant or dramatic, I stood by while the police handled details and the body was removed. I moved a few things, made some phone calls, and tried to calm the mother.
>
> When I left at midnight, I didn't think I'd been very helpful

or comforting. I felt guilty that I'd not known what to do, so I continued visiting this family as the weeks went on. Whenever I could, I'd drop in and say hello.

As time passed, the son came to trial. It seemed inevitable that he'd be convicted of murder. I planned to sit with the family at the trial. But one day I received a phone call informing me that the son had killed himself. Although I knew I needed to be with the family, once again I felt totally inadequate to meet their needs. What could I say? What could I do?

I spent time with the parents, listened to their thoughts and fears, and offered them my compassion. In the months that followed, I kept going to see the family, just sitting and visiting with them and letting them talk.

One day, the father looked up and told me, "Chaplain, we want to thank you for the time you've spent with us and all that you've done for us. I don't know how we'd have made it through all this if it hadn't been for you."

I didn't know I'd done anything that was either right or helpful. All I knew was that I kept going to see them. I was willing to sit with them and be part of their grief. This taught me very early in my ministerial career that it's not important to have big speeches prepared or to do major things, but rather to be there.[2]

~ 26 ~

The Art of a Thank-You Note

Choose a good reputation over great riches; being held in high esteem is better than silver or gold.

—Proverbs 22:1 nlt

One of the kindest things you can do is to express your gratitude with a handwritten thank-you note. It's a tangible way to say you're grateful for being treated well. Some consider such correspondence as only for the female gender, but that's a manner myth. Men and women both need to take time from their hectic schedules to express appreciation for kindnesses extended to them.

Don't limit your thank-you notes to those who have given you a gift. Think about the list of people you could thank—someone who hosted you overnight, a pastor who gave an inspirational sermon, those who sent you a get-well card, an employer who gave you a bonus, someone who has done an exceptional job, or someone who has offered time and energy to counsel you when hurting. Anyone who has been a friend, a help, or a comfort can be thanked in this way. The list is endless; it goes on and on.

We love getting a thank-you note, but we're not quite as excited to take the time required to write and send one. We have good intentions to, but then life gets busy, and the notes drop on our priority list. When I was so sick with cancer, I didn't have the energy to send out notes for all the kind letters, gifts, and well wishes that I received.

My husband, Bob, was so touched by the generosity of our friends, prayer partners, and strangers that he personally wrote hundreds of cards thanking them for sending us a card, having flowers delivered, bringing food over, and visiting me while in the hospital. Many people commented that their hearts were touched by seeing how we communicated our thankfulness. Men shared with Bob that they were shown how to respond if their wives ever became sick.

We discovered how meaningful a note can be from a woman whose father had passed away. At his funeral she came up to us and shared that while she was going through some of her father's papers, she noticed a note from my husband tacked to his message board. My Bob had written to her dad and expressed that he was praying for him as he went through a difficult period a few years previous. A thank-you note my husband sent was so inspirational to her dad that he saved it on his wall to be displayed and reread for encouragement. We should never underestimate what a note means to another person. Take the time to share your life with another.

Failure to write a thank-you note can affect your reputation. Not sending a note of appreciation will certainly be noted and remembered—and remembered for a long time.

The ungrateful person is one who is unable to give
back a little joy that was received or experienced.
—ANDRÉ COMTE-SPONVILLE

We all want people to think of us in a positive light. The two minutes it takes for you to write a note will come back to you tenfold. These notes illustrate your thoughtfulness, good manners, and your classiness. Besides, you feel good when you return goodness with goodness.

When Do You Send a Thank-You Note?

- for all wedding gifts
- for other-occasion gifts

- for being an overnight guest in someone's home
- for parties you attend
- for kind acts given to you
- for hosting you to a lunch or dinner
- for those who sent flowers or donations to the funeral of one of your family members

When in doubt, send a thank-you card. You can never go wrong by going the extra mile. Even though your social circle may not be accustomed to sending out notes of appreciation, the recipient would be pleased by your expression of gratitude.

What to Say

A note can be very brief, but it should include several elements:

1. a mention of the gift itself
2. an expression of its beauty and how well it was presented
3. a mention of how you like the gift and how you will use it
4. a final remark of greetings or affection
5. your signature

Make your note sound like you. You don't need to use words or phrases that are not normally in your vocabulary. Many people avoid writing thank-you notes because they are intimidated by the thought of sounding formal or stuffy. Just be your grateful self.

When to Mail Your Notes

The sooner the better. Try to get a note in the mail shortly after receiving the gift or upon receiving the act of kindness. Most etiquette experts allow two weeks to mail thank-you notes—other than wedding gifts. To help shorten the gap and the number of thank-you cards for a wedding gift, you might get an early start by writing your notes early for those gifts sent to your home. This will greatly help you get a head start. However, your wedding notes should be no later than two months from the ceremony. It is better to send them out as early as possible.

*A smile of encouragement at the right moment
may act like sunlight on a closed-up flower; it
may be the turning point for a struggling life.*

—UNKNOWN

The Art of Conversation

A good listener is not only popular everywhere,
but after a while he gets to know something.

—WILSON MIZNER

Good conversation lets you be a creative artist every time you speak—or listen. The key to being a good conversationalist is to listen at least as much as you talk. Good conversation is as much about being quiet and listening as it is about speaking words.

Not only do good conversationalists listen, they also don't ramble, don't gossip, and don't bore. They work to understand the other person's views. Etiquette and manners are not out-of-date rules. They're accepted guidelines for making others comfortable.

Good conversation does not include these:

- confessing
- scolding
- interviewing
- notifying
- debating
- giving instructions
- shouting

- giving insults
- talking over one another

Tools for Good Conversation

You can learn to make the best use of your voice, facial expressions, and body language. Your smile, your humor, your posture, and the way you dress also impact how you will come across. Remember, the first impression one gets about you is so very important. Sometimes you never get a second chance.

How you introduce yourself to someone influences the rest of your visit. For example, I can start with: "Hello, my name is Emilie" or "I'm Emilie (or Emilie Barnes)" or "I'd like to introduce myself to you, I'm Emilie." After the introduction you might extend your hand for a handshake.

How to Remember Names

A gifted conversationalist remembers every name, every time. With a little help and some practice, you can too. Here are some helpful hints:

- Gather your wits before you meet a new group of people. If you can, do your homework ahead of time by reviewing or thinking through a list of names that you will then connect to faces.

- When you're introduced to someone, say their name out loud as you greet them and make eye contact. Say their name at least once during the conversation, and say it again when you part. This will help it sink in to your memory.

- Say the name over a few times in your mind and link it to a visual image. If her name is Mary Jane, imagine her wearing Mary Jane shoes. Or connect the person with others who have that name; visualize the Ben Lincoln you've just met standing next to Abe Lincoln.

- Use rhyming: "Tall Paul" or "Nate the waiter." (Just don't say it out loud.)

- Follow up. Reinforce your memory by looking at his name tag, asking him for a card, and writing his name down as soon as you get home.[1]

What to Do When Your Mind Goes Blank

At one time or the other we draw a blank when we see someone and need to introduce them to another person. Help! What do you do?

- Be upfront and honest. Say something like, "I know we've met before, and I remember the occasion. Could you remind me of your name?" Or, "I am Emilie, and we know each other from the past." Or, "We're both friends of Jenny's." Or, "I'm sorry, my mind is going blank. I remember you, but I can't remember your name."

- Invite another friend into the conversation so that they might reveal the person's name. For example, if you brought your son into the social circle, you could say, "Let me introduce you to my son Brad." The person whose name you can't remember will then be able to introduce himself to Brad. When this exchange happens, be sure to pay close attention to the person's name.

- I'm over 50, so I have a very good excuse: "I'm having a senior moment. Could you help me remember your name?"

- Don't be afraid to use pen and paper: "Let me write your name down so I'll recall your name for our next meeting."

- Business cards are a wonderful way to find out a person's name. When you get home, place it in your business card folder for future reference.

- Don't risk guessing a person's name. It's better to admit that you need help than to call a person by the wrong name.

- If you do forget a person's name or reference the wrong name, there is no need to apologize more than once. Get on with the conversation.

Be a Good Listener

Don't feel that you have to fill in the silent spaces with run-on chatter. You become a good talker by being a good listener, so try out these ideas:

- Listen attentively when others are talking.
- Keep good eye contact with the one speaking. Keep your body language under control.
- Smile. Nod your head in agreement occasionally so the talker knows you're still listening and interested.
- Only interrupt when it's an appropriate response. Most people like to talk about their interests.

How to Move a Conversation Along

Be aware of the amount of time you're talking to another person at a party or business meeting. You want to be sensitive not to take up too much time with one person—even if you're having a good conversation. There are several polite ways to make the break.

Change your body language and use kind phrases such as these:

- "It's been nice talking to you."
- "I've really enjoyed catching up on your life."
- "Please excuse me, I must be moving on."
- "I'm glad we had the opportunity to meet."
- "I need to excuse myself to visit the restroom."
- "Let's go over to the buffet and get some food and beverage."
- "I need to look after a few of the guests who I haven't visited with."

- "I need to circulate with the crowd."
- "I'm going outside to get a fresh breath of air. Please excuse me."
- "Do you have a card? I'd like to contact you later."

Shared laughter creates a bond of friendship. When people laugh together, they cease to be young and old, master and pupils, worker and driver. They have become a single group of human beings, enjoying their existence.

—WILLIAM GRANT LEE

~ 28 ~

Dating Manners

'Tis better to have loved and lost
than never to have loved at all.

—Lord Alfred Tennyson

The standards for proper manners regarding dating and courtship have certainly changed over the past 20 years. However, a few good guidelines can still help people through this process.

What Is a Date?

A date is between a man and a woman who plan on getting together at a specified time to do something special. It's a date when someone asks you to go to a football game, a movie, to church, on a picnic, horseback riding, and the like.

A date could be a formal event or something as casual as going out for coffee or ice cream, going rollerblading, or taking a walk on the beach.

It is still proper for the man to ask directly or on the telephone for that first encounter. Women, hold back and let the man take the leadership. Even though many women today call to ask and set a date, the man would prefer to do the asking.

If you happen to be shy and aren't really sure about being alone with the other person, plan to double date. It takes a lot of pressure off of you until you get to know the person a little bit better. In today's culture it's a safer way in which to initially get to know someone.

Dating Manners

- Give someone a call at least three days before you want to set a time and day. This gives a little lead time to get your hair and nails done or for the gentleman to get his favorite outfit from the cleaners.

- Make that first date one that is a match for the other party's interests. A movie if they like a movie, a baseball game if they like sports, or a walk on the beach or a trail hike if they are athletic.

- Try not to change plans at the last minute.

- Be on time.

- Dress for the occasion. After all, you want to make a good impression.

- Be sensitive to the other person's budget. The gentleman is the one to pay for the date. Even if a woman wants to split the costs, the gentleman is the one to pay for the expenses of the date.

- Keep the conversation on upbeat topics.

- If you don't feel well or if you are tired, try to be positive in your attitude.

- At the end of the evening, express a heartfelt thank-you for the evening, even if the chemistry wasn't too positive between the two of you.

- Try to laugh and have a pleasant sense of humor.

- If the date is going in the wrong direction, you have the right to excuse yourself from the date. If you grow uncomfortable with your date's behavior, take whatever steps are necessary to escape from the situation, whether that means calling a cab, asking the restaurant manager to help you, or calling the police if the situation becomes difficult. This probably won't happen, but if it does, act upon it. Trust your instincts.

- If the person wants to see you again and you would like to have another date, you can certainly say yes. If, however, you weren't on the same wavelength and you don't wish for another date, you might as well nip it in the bud and say, "No, I don't think that would be a good idea." It's okay to be firm and frank. Be courteous but direct.

What About a Blind Date?

When the idea of a blind date comes up, some people say, "No way, not me!" However, a blind date can be a great way to meet someone. Who knows, this next date might be with the one who suits you. Even though the last 20 blind dates went south, the twenty-first one might be the winner—give it a try. Here are some good attitudes to have when approaching a date with someone you don't know:

- Whoever is trying to fix you up usually has your best interest at heart. They only want to fix you up with a winner. After all, they want the best for you.

- Countless couples who met on a blind date are happily married today. Who knows, you could be part of that statistic.

- The blind date might not be your style, but maybe the friend of the blind date would be a better match for you.

- A blind date might take you on a grand adventure—somewhere you would not normally visit. Enjoy this chance to try something new and get to know someone.

- Even negative first impressions can turn into a positive experience. Wait until the evening is over before you make that final judgment.

Calling Off the Romance

One date can turn into a dating relationship that lasts for weeks, months, and even years. There might be a time when it's obvious to one or both partners that they need to stop the dating and romance experience. What is the best way to handle this difficult part of romance? It's best to break up the dating of two unmarried people than to break up a marriage five years later when lives are very invested in the effort and when children might be involved.

Good manners can help this time in your life. They show that you are simply being sensitive to and concerned about other people's welfare and feelings. Remember to abide by the Golden Rule. If you are the person walking out of the relationship, you have a responsibility to show as much compassion as possible.

- State to all your friends that the breakup was a mutually-agreed-upon development.
- Never criticize the other person in public.
- Come to a mutual agreement if there are any financial obligations to consider.
- Be kind as you enter into a relationship, be kind in the relationship, and be kind as you exit the relationship.

Love cannot be forced, Love cannot be coaxed and teased, It comes out of heaven, Unasked and unsought.

—PEARL BUCK

A Tea Party Has Its Own Etiquette

*Thank God for tea! What would the
world do without tea? How did it exist?
I am glad I was not born before tea.*

—Reverend Sidney Smith

Serving tea is a wonderful way to sharpen etiquette around the table. Mothers can use this time to instruct their daughters about the importance of learning and practicing good manners when they are invited to a tea. Friends can also teach each other the art of the proper tea party while enjoying the fellowship that goes with such a gathering. Here are some guidelines that will help you exhibit your best manners.

- The server of tea (and all liquids) serves from the right. The person being served holds her cup in her right hand. You may adjust this if the person receiving the beverage is left-handed.

- To prevent getting lipstick on your tea cup, blot your lips before you sit down at the serving table.

- Scones and crumpets should be eaten in small pieces. If butter, jam, or cream cheese is used, add them to each piece as it is eaten.

- Good manners will dictate proper conversation. Good topics include theater, museums, fine arts, music, movies, literature, and travel. Stay away from politics, religion, aches and pains, deaths, and negative discussion. Keep the conversation upbeat.

- A knife and fork are usually used with open-faced sandwiches and cakes with icing. A spoon is used to stir your teacup (particularly helpful if you are adding cream or lemon flavor).

- It's not proper to reach across someone else's body when you want something off the table. Politely ask for someone at the table to "Please pass the _____."

- When passing food around the table, always pass to the right.

- Use your napkin to wipe your mouth after drinking a liquid or eating a gooey dessert.

- If you must excuse yourself from the serving table, say very politely, "Please excuse me." Place your napkin on the seat of your chair, indicating that you will be coming back. However, if you're excusing yourself from the table and not returning to your seat, place the napkin on the table to the right of your plate. This will indicate to the hostess or server that you are finished and that she may clear your plate.

- Dress appropriately for the occasion. A tea requires something dainty and feminine. Casual clothes aren't recommended. It's better to be overdressed than underdressed.

Etiquette for the Guest

The hostess has guidelines to follow in order to create a wonderful event. When you're the guest and you embrace mannerly behavior, the gathering is more enjoyable for everyone. And your hostess will be glad she invited you. Here are some tips to help you become a model guest.

- Bring the hostess a small gift.
- Be punctual, but not early.

- Cancel only in an emergency.
- Offer to help the hostess if help is needed.
- Be a good mixer with the other guests.
- If the tea has a theme, dress according to the theme. It will add a special touch to the event.
- Even if you enjoy talking and socializing, try not to be the last to leave.
- Be sure to say a goodbye to the hostess.
- Write a thank-you note within 24 hours of the party.

Food Placement for a Three-Tier Curate Stand

The protocol of placing the scones on the top tier began during the 1800s, when afternoon tea first became popular and modern kitchen conveniences did not exist. A warming dome was placed over the scones and would fit only on the top tier. The savories and tea sandwiches were placed on the middle tier, followed by the sweets on the bottom. At the progression of each course, service would be provided to remove each tier.

Tea Brings Out the Best Manners

There's something about a table set for tea that brings out the best manners in anyone. The social graces that mothers try to instill in their children are likely to emerge when a proper situation presents itself. Children of all ages treat the special ritual of teatime with reverence.

"Would you like some tea?"

"Yes, please."

"Would you like sugar?"

"Yes. Thank you very much."

Such simple exchanges embody the true spirit of the tea party. You see, serving tea is a peaceful moment of reciprocation. At a table covered in white lace and adorned with delicate cups, I learned to respect people. I learned how to listen, to share, to offer and receive.

Tea presents an atmosphere where the give and take of a relation-ship—the ebb and flow of kindness and care—sets the rhythm for the moment.

And when I am alone, cozy in a chair with a blanket draped over my lap and a cup of tea on the side table, the same swell of gratitude fills me. Here too I take a moment to listen, to share, to offer and receive.

And most important of all, I say thank you.[1]

A Teatime Tidbit

If you enjoy chocolate and mint, heat a cup of milk with a mint teabag then stir in a little hot cocoa mix. Serve as is, or garnish with a dollop of whipped topping.

At times our own light goes out and is rekindled by a spark from another person. Each of us has cause to think with deep gratitude of those who have lighted the flame within us.

—ALBERT SCHWEITZER

Wediquette Etiquette: Part One

*Often the difference between a successful
marriage and a mediocre one consists of
leaving three or four things a day unsaid.*

—HARLAN MILLER

It's so wonderful to know that people are still getting married. This sacred bond between a man, a woman, and God is still in vogue. There's something magical about a would-be bride who has been thinking about her special day since she was 15 years old. She can tell you in detail about the groom, the church setting, her wedding dress, who will be in attendance on the big day, and the flavor of the multitiered cake.[1]

Over the years proper "wediquette" has changed. Every wedding seems to be unique. But a few common principles should be used in planning and performing the wedding. There are also principles of good behavior for those in attendance.

Knowing what is proper helps one make choices based on knowledge rather than guesswork. It helps to ask a lot of questions when one decides to get married. The easier tasks are those that deal with logistics, such as finding the pastor, the church, the caterer, and the photographers. The hardest job is dealing with family emotions and needs. The future bride has her ideas, and so do the two moms. They too have envisioned this day.

Making good decisions is the key to maintaining good relationships during the planning of such an event—after all, this will probably be the largest party that either family will host. Often the bride and her parents make most of the decisions. A wise bride will do well to solicit feedback from the groom and his parents. It is an important moment in the history and legacy of both families!

Different cultures and nationalities have varying views about what is to be included in a wedding, so the bride and the groom need to discuss these differences before a wedding is to be planned. Good communication is very necessary. Thankfully, some of the most important, time-honored conventions of weddings remain the same. Most cultures recognize that marriage is the most important step a man and a woman can take and that society benefits from the solid structure that this union brings about. It provides protection for the children, a link to the past of both families, and a respect between the bride and groom as they live out their love for each other. Marriage brings a sense of security to the couple that decides to marry.

The Engagement

The chemistry between a man and woman changes when they announce, "We're going to get married!" Everyone around them knows this couple is serious—no longer just daters. The phones start ringing, the women start screaming, and the men can't figure out what everyone's excited about.

The future bride and her parents will be busy writing notes to close friends, and they, in turn, pass on the good news to others. It is common courtesy for the bride's mother to wait to hear from the young man's mother and talk about the upcoming wedding *before* she calls the newspaper to arrange for the announcement to be printed in the paper. During this conversation, they will schedule a time both sets of parents can get together to talk over the plans for this big upcoming event. And they will express how excited they are to receive the bride and groom into their families.

In most cases, the bride's mother will take the initiative to get details started since the bride's parents are responsible for most aspects of the wedding. If the groom's parents are divorced, the protocol should be the same—the bride's mother calls the parents with whom the groom lives. The mother is contacted first, then the father.

The Engagement Party

Generally the bride's parents host the engagement party. However, others may extend the offer to host, and it is appropriate to accept such an offer. This is a great way for both families to meet and to honor the future bride and groom.

If the groom's family lives out of town, they may want to plan a separate engagement party in their area. If so, they should extend the invitation to the bride's parents and family.

There will be circumstances when the parents of both parties meet for the first time at the wedding. If at all possible, a meeting prior to festivities is preferable. This helps ease tension and jitters on the wedding day.

An Engagement Ring

Do I or don't I? That is the question. The groom must decide when to get the engagement ring for his bride-to-be. It's generally accepted that in this engagement period the future groom will offer a diamond ring when he asks the future bride to be his wife. It is generally acceptable to have the jeweler resize the ring and to change the ring if the design or setting is not agreeable for everyone.

Oftentimes the bride and groom will have discussed and shopped for engagement and wedding rings during their courtship, thus establishing which style of ring is the best match. Here are a few tips to help make the engagement ring selection easier:

- Stay within your budget according to your lifestyle and economic level.

- Make sure your sales receipt states the ring is purchased "on approval."

- The engagement ring of a matching set is worn above the wedding band.

- Rings can be adjusted to size.

Engagement and Wedding Announcements

Some will say, "Yes, it's proper to send out printed announcements for the engagement and the wedding," and some will say, "No, use the newspaper announcement for both." It is important to think through this delicate matter. If you use the newspaper, no one feels obligated to send gifts. It also helps you to avoid possible confusion—when people receive an engagement announcement, they might assume they'll receive a wedding invitation, and that's not always the case.

As a couple, you and your parents should discuss and do what you feel comfortable with. If you do choose to use the local newspaper to make the announcement, you will furnish the pictures and written information. This way you can control the names, spellings, and basic information. Giving information over the telephone is dangerous. Often the details are printed with errors. You might consider having wedding announcements in the hometown newspaper where you and your family grew up.

Gifts

Gifts are tokens of goodwill, affection, and commitment. Just because you are invited to a lavish wedding doesn't mean you have to give a lavish gift. Presents should be within one's means.

All gifts should be sent to the bride's home before the wedding. After the wedding, gifts go either to the bridal couple's home or to the bride's parents' home. Bringing gifts to the wedding should be minimized. All those gifts have to be handled and transported to a planned destination on the day of the wedding. The couple already has enough details for the day.

Knowing Who Sent What

A little planning and organization will help you keep an accurate record of gifts that arrive before the wedding. The bride or groom can't possibly remember who gave what. A list is necessary. Record the name of the sender, what was given, the date it arrived, and the date you sent the thank-you note. If you receive gifts at the wedding or at a later time, that same information is added to the list.

Gifts of Money

In days past, money was not given as a gift unless it was from a parent or a very close relative or friend. However, today there seems to be more flexibility on this matter. If money is given at the wedding it should be given in a very discreet fashion—checks remain unopened and are given to the bride's father or to the best man for safekeeping.

Exchanging Gifts

The returning or exchanging of wedding gifts should be handled in a very discreet fashion. If the gift you want to exchange is from someone who will be visiting your home and would notice whether the gift was there or not, you might politely discuss the situation with them. However, if the gift is from someone you won't be entertaining in your home, feel free to exchange it. The same is true for duplicate gifts.

Thank-You Notes

Whether you respond with a timely thank-you note for gifts given at the engagement party or the wedding will influence the way people think of you. Grateful people give thanks. It's very important that this form of etiquette be done in a timely manner. Thank-you notes for engagement party gifts should be sent out within three weeks. Wedding thank-you notes should go out within two months after you return from the honeymoon.

Gifts for Attendants

The bride has her obligations and the groom has his. The bride pays for her bridesmaids' gifts and the groom pays for those who serve him. These gifts are given as a gesture of appreciation for making the wonderful occasion. They need to be personal, but they don't have to be costly. Many stores will give you a discount for buying several gifts at a time. Here are a few ideas for bridesmaids:

> perfume
>
> earrings
>
> bracelet
>
> necklace (cross)
>
> pewter picture frame
>
> brooch

These are some ideas for groomsmen:

> money clip
>
> tie clasp
>
> leather wallet
>
> pen and pencil set
>
> desk clock
>
> business card holder

The maid or matron of honor as well as the best man should receive slightly more expensive gifts because their duties for the day are more involved.

Gifts to Parents

It is very proper to give each of the bride and groom's parents a token gift in appreciation for all they've done to raise you to this event in your life. If you plan to purchase these on your honeymoon, let your parents know of your plans.

> *The man who finds a wife finds a treasure,*
> *and he receives favor from the Lord.*
>
> —PROVERBS 18:22 NLT

31

Wediquette Etiquette: Part Two

*Praise marriage not on the third
day, but after the third year.*

—UNKNOWN

A wedding involves so many details that a second chapter is required! The questions and considerations for a wedding can be overwhelming, but they are a part of a significant, exciting milestone that is worth the effort. The following sections address more wedding details and the best way to manage them.

Guest Lists

The wedding day is the bride's day! The bride's family members are considered the hosts for this event, so they will decide the number of guests to be invited. The tricky part is to determine how many to invite and how to divide the number between the two families. Is it 50/50, or will the host family invite more guests than the groom's parents because they are funding the expenses? If the groom's side of the wedding wants more invitations than they are allocated, the bride's parents have a few alternatives:

- Give some of their allotment to the groom's family.
- Say no—they will have to work within their number.

- Say yes and expand the size of the wedding.
- Say yes but stipulate that the groom's parents will have to assume the extra costs for their guests.

The host family will have to make that decision. In some cases, the groom's parents will be the host family. Budget limitations may play a factor in that decision. Practical hosts must be able to make hard decisions—they may have to allot a certain number of guests and adhere to that number. When budget and size of facility determine how many guests there will be, you might consider having two lists:

- those invited to the ceremony only
- those invited to the ceremony and to the reception following the ceremony

Some couples might feel uncomfortable with a double list. However, this practice has become more and more common in recent years. If the family belongs to a church and invites the whole congregation, the family might invite the church to the ceremony only, reserving the reception event to immediate family and personal friends.

Creating guest lists can be a difficult and trying time. No one wants to offend family members or friends. No matter what you decide, you will offend someone. Don't let that worry you, but remember that you cannot please everyone. Don't put that pressure on yourself.

Invitations

The choices on style and expense for invitations are as broad as your budget will allow. You can go from the high end of copperplate engraving etched with fine line lettering to the least expensive method of flat printing, on which the ink looks darker. Tastes vary and expenses vary. You will have to come to some agreement on what price range you can handle. The main factors you'll face when creating your invitation are these:

style of typeset

costs of printing

proper wording

color of ink

matching envelopes

If you aren't the bride, be sure to include the bride and groom when making these decisions. Each generation has its own unique style of what's good and what's not. Mom may like something that's entirely different than what the daughter likes. The good news is that there are many styles to choose from now. It is tough to pare down the choices, but in the end you'll be very pleased with the selection.

The printer will have sample wordings to help you match your type of wedding: traditional, divorced parents with joint invitations, a double wedding, a single parent, a divorcée, a wedding hosted by the bridegroom's parents, a military wedding, or whatever else might be your situation. Don't hesitate to use the expertise of printers.

Before you go to press, make sure you proof the wording—misprints do happen! It's better to take a few extra minutes to look over each detail carefully than to be in a hurry and let the opportunity pass you by.

It's customary to send invitations out at least three weeks ahead of the time. If you have guests from out of state or foreign countries, more lead time would be recommended.

The invited guest should respond within ten days of receiving the invitation—always RSVP.

Who would think that there is a proper way to stuff an envelope? But it's true. The first consideration is to put yourself in the recipient's position. How would you like to open an envelope? You first should see the handwritten names on the unsealed inner envelope. As you carefully turn the unsealed envelope over to withdraw the invitation, the engraved wording should face you. If you have any enclosures, they should be in front of or placed inside the fold of the invitation—this way nothing will be overlooked.

Considerations for Planning the Wedding

The more time and detail you put in at the front end, the less confusion and stress will occur as you get closer to the date. If your budget permits, you might consider hiring an experienced wedding coordinator who can prevent certain pitfalls. She can also help make decisions to suit your tastes and preferences. This can be a real lifesaver. If you can't afford such a person, consult with friends who have had this experience. Check out books from the library, go online, and interview the gown provider, the caterer, and the baker. They have had vast experience and can offer exceptional insight. It's very important not to operate on assumptions—this can create misunderstandings or an end result that doesn't suit the goals and dreams of the bride and groom. It's most important that a mother and daughter are in agreement. It is courteous to include the groom's mother so she will feel involved.

Before you get too far in the planning process, you must consider three very important questions:

1. How formal will it be?
2. What is the budget?
3. How many guests will be invited?

You cannot have a very formal wedding on a small budget. This type of wedding will have a more expensive wedding dress, more flowers, more attendants, more outside costs for housing out-of-area guests, and so on. Formal isn't for everyone. It doesn't suit every budget or personal style. Set the boundaries in the very beginning. If you do this, you'll end up with an event that is everything you want it to be. A very casual wedding can be great fun and very romantic when set at the beach, in a garden, or at a ski resort with only a small group of intimate family and friends invited. Most importantly, a wedding should be a happy experience for everyone, especially the bride and groom and their parents.

Clergy

The selection of the clergy is the responsibility of the bride and her parents. If the groom would like to have his clergy included, you need to arrange early in the planning so those arrangements can be made.

In most cases, the bridegroom will be responsible to pay the clergy's honorarium. Check around your area to see what the recommended amount may be. Each denomination has different policies on how they handle weddings. Some feel that such events are part of their ministering to the members of their congregation. Others consider weddings as a means for them to add to their salary. Some may not charge for their services but would appreciate you donating monies to their church or synagogue.

If the clergy travels to perform the ceremony, the bridegroom needs to pay for any travel, food, or housing expenses. The main point is to be appreciative for the services rendered.

Marriage License

Every state has its own requirements for obtaining a marriage license. Check with your local officials to see what their requirements are. To be legally married, you must obtain a marriage license. It certifies that...

- You're both of legal age to be married (or have parental consent).
- You have met all necessary requirements such as blood tests and perhaps a waiting period.
- You both are single, widowed, or divorced.

This license shows the one officiating the wedding that you have been cleared by the state agency and that he or she can lawfully marry you. After the wedding ceremony the person officiating the nuptial event, the bridal couple, and two witnesses will sign the marriage license to prove that the marriage has taken place.

The Wedding Day

This is the day everyone has anticipated for many years. If good planning skills have been used, it should be a day of calmness—for the most part. The bride will look the best she ever has looked and the groom will be at his handsomest. Flowers will be in full bloom, the music will echo in the church, a young child will spread rose petals down the aisle, the wedding court will be dressed in their finest— everyone is anticipating this occasion.

As a final check, make sure you have:

> marriage license
>
> wedding rings
>
> passports, if needed
>
> airplane tickets, if needed
>
> extra hosiery for the bride
>
> car keys
>
> money
>
> credit cards
>
> toiletries for bride and groom

No matter how exciting the day is, be calm—and know that you're surrounded by those who love and adore you.

Paying Expenses

Historically, the bride's parents have paid for the complete wedding. The thinking behind this concept is that the groom will take on the obligation for the expenses that are incurred in raising a family. However, in today's culture, the bride often has a career and will contribute to the future household expenses. Many couples today make arrangements with both sets of parents to help offset the wedding expenses. However, it's wise never to assume such. At the early stage of wedding planning, the two sets of parents need to discuss what is expected and what can be anticipated. You certainly don't want to create any lifelong hard feelings because you neglected to have a conversation. Talking about money isn't a favorite activity for most folks, but this discussion can be pleasant and can help unite the families in a common goal.

Here are a few guidelines, but keep in mind that every marriage ceremony has its own unique situation.

Traditional Expenses for the Bride and Her Family

- invitations and wedding announcements
- wedding ceremony, including music, the house of worship, and flowers
- wedding reception, including music, food, wedding cake, gratuities
- flowers carried by bride's attendants
- bride's wedding dress and accessories and personal trousseau
- bridegroom's wedding band for a double-ring ceremony
- bridesmaids' gifts
- bridesmaids' luncheon
- stationery for handwritten thank-you notes and other correspondence
- wedding gift book and guest book
- photographs (both formal and candid), photograph albums, and videography
- transportation for the wedding party
- accommodations for out-of-town members of the bride's wedding party

Traditional Wedding Expenses for the Bridegroom and His Parents

- bride's engagement and wedding rings
- marriage license
- boutonnieres for father and male attendants
- bride's bouquet if customary in your region
- bride's going-away corsage
- flowers for both mothers and grandmothers
- wedding gift for the bride
- gifts for ushers and best man
- bachelor dinner (optional)
- officiant's fee
- transportation for the bridal couple
- wardrobe
- honeymoon (unless it is given as a wedding gift)
- family's traveling expenses
- lodgings for out-of-town attendants
- wedding gift to the couple
- rehearsal dinner [1]

Bridesmaids' and Groomsmen's Expenses

- wedding clothes
- travel costs
- individual gift to the couple or a share of a collective gift
- bridesmaids also pay for a shower gift

When to Depart

The grand day has to wind down at some point. Eventually it's time to think about departing from the reception. There doesn't seem to be any set rules for this occasion. Each wedding party has its own chemistry.

Some couples might prefer to be the last ones to leave, and other couples might have planes to catch for their honeymoons. If you're wondering about when the gifts should be opened, the answer is "later." Gifts are best opened privately by the bride and groom. Many gifts are sent in advance of the event, so there is no way to properly represent all the gifts given if they are opened at the event. And the amount spent on each gift varies. You never want people to feel badly about the gift they have given. Save that enjoyable task for a special moment as husband and wife. Some couples open gifts while in the presence of their parents if a lot of friends of the family attended and gave presents.

The party isn't over just because the new husband and wife need to leave the reception. The parents can excuse themselves for a few minutes so they can say their goodbyes, then they will return for continued festivities of the evening.

Often the best man might signal to the audience that the bride and groom will be departing in a few minutes, and those wishing can assemble and make two rows leading from the exit to their getaway car. At this time rice or birdseed might be tossed by friends and family to send them off with cheers and clapping.

Many newlyweds will want to stay in a hotel locally for the night rather than travel after such a hectic day.

Whenever a bride and groom decide to leave, they'll leave gracefully and with hearts of thanksgiving for a wonderful wedding day.

Father God, as we gather for
the wedding of _____
we bring them to You as a couple who have
put their faith in Your leadership for their
lives. May they always look to You for
direction and guidance. May they always be
committed to the vows that they have made to
You this day. We who are gathered together
offer our prayers and encouragement to help
them along the way of becoming one in spirit.
Bless their lives abundantly. Amen.

32

Being a Gracious Adult

We are haunted by an ideal life, and it is because
we have within us the beginning and possibility of it.

—PHILLIPS BROOKS

This checklist is just a midterm checkup on how you're doing in being an adult with manners. Fortunately, it isn't the final exam. Often we aren't even aware of our sins of omission. Hopefully these items will jog your mind to be more aware and sensitive to areas in which you have become lax.

1. Are you on time for appointments? Do you return phone calls and e-mails in a timely manner?
   Yes   No

2. When making telephone calls, do you acknowledge yourself and determine if you are interrupting?
   Yes   No

3. Do you pick up after yourself at meetings and social engagements?
   Yes   No

4. Do you handle RSVPs on a timely basis?
   Yes   No

5. Do you regularly express gratitude and send notes of thanks?
   Yes   No

6. Do you notice people in lines ahead of and behind you and look for opportunities to be courteous?
Yes   No

7. Do you hold the door for others and offer to carry packages for them?
Yes   No

8. Do you notice a "mother of the faith" and offer her a chair or place in line before you?
Yes   No

9. Do you maintain good eye contact? Do you keep from looking down or over the head of the person to whom you are speaking?
Yes   No

10. Do you avoid finishing others' sentences?
Yes   No

11. Do you listen to people?
Yes   No

12. Do you treat people as equals regardless of their appearance?
Yes   No

13. Do you avoid interrupting people?
Yes   No

14. Do you enter and exit conversations appropriately?
Yes   No

15. Do you acknowledge the people who are in your immediate presence?
Yes   No

16. How are your table manners? Do you finish the last of a dish without offering it to others?
Yes   No

17. Do you know which fork to use?
    Yes   No

18. Do you use a napkin and place it on your lap?
    Yes   No

19. Do you avoid speaking with your mouth full?
    Yes   No

20. Do you eat at a relaxed pace and finish when your host does?
    Yes   No

21. Do you wait for your hostess to determine when it is time to eat?
    Yes   No

22. Do you avoid reaching in front of others?
    Yes   No

23. Are you the first to yield to an ambulance or other emergency vehicle?
    Yes   No

24. Do you speak loudly and clearly enough for older people to hear and understand you?
    Yes   No

25. When traveling, do you note and care for other passengers?
    Yes   No

26. Do you avoid road rage and negative self-talk in the car?
    Yes   No

27. Do you introduce yourself at social gatherings?
    Yes   No

28. Do you use titles appropriately (such as Sir, Miss, and Mrs.)?[1]
    Yes   No

    Total of each: Yes_____   No _____

20–23 yeses: You are well mannered and will receive a lot of invitations.

16–19 yeses: You're trying, but still need to do a lot of work.

12–15 yeses: Consider going back to chapter 1 and starting again.

0–11 yeses: You may not be invited to too many parties!

Extra Credit

- What personal habits do you have that may intrude on others in public (such as bouncing your leg, blowing your nose loudly, or laughing or talking loudly)?
- How often do you use *my, me,* or *I* in conversation?
- How is your theater etiquette?
- How is your church etiquette?

Have you had a kindness shown? Pass it on;
'Twas not given for thee alone, Pass it on;
Let it travel down the years,
Let it wipe another's tears.
Pass it on.

—REV. HENRY BURTON

~ 33 ~

Out-and-About Manners

*Only when one is connected to one's
own core is one connected to others.*

—ANNE MORROW LINDBERGH

We should be concerned about being proper not only within our homes but also when we are out and about. We come across situations that don't fall into typical etiquette scenarios. This chapter addresses those guidelines for the not-so-usual settings.

As a Pedestrian and Driver

Most cities mark their streets with white lines at the crosswalks. Large cities have problems with jaywalkers. These inconsiderate walkers cause all kinds of problems. There are good reasons not to be a jaywalker: It's against the law, many people are killed while jaywalking, it causes drivers to slam on their brakes to avoid hitting the walker, tempers flare—words are exchanged, and road rage can result.

The proper behavior is to cross the street at designated crosswalks—and don't forget to wait for the signal to turn green before stepping off the curb.

- As a driver, yield when pedestrians are in the crosswalk. Remain patient and calm even if you will be delayed a minute or two.

- When you're parking your car, be considerate of others who have parked their cars. When parallel parking, leave enough room between the cars so the car ahead and behind you can get out of their spaces without bumping or damaging your car. Also, be considerate not to use more parking space than you need. Leave enough room for others to park if space permits. If you're parking in a mall setting, be sure to leave enough space between cars so the drivers of the cars next to you can enter their cars and exit. Many mall parking spaces are for compact cars.

- Avoid using the horn when you become irritated by another motorist. Many cities are known for their short-fused motorists. Stay calm and wait a few extra seconds. Often the person you honk your horn at can't do anything about the delay ahead of them.

- Many vehicles have their headlights on day and night. Usually high beams during the day don't cause any problems; however, make sure you drive with low beams during the nighttime. The approaching cars will certainly appreciate your courtesy. High beams are fine for the wide-open spaces, but go to the lows when there is oncoming traffic.

- Slow drivers need to drive in the appropriate lane so they won't bog down the faster moving traffic. Avoid staying in the fast lanes—this causes the faster vehicles to continually switch lanes. Switching lanes is the number one reason for accidents on the highway.

- Be thoughtful enough to use your turn signals when making a lane change. Allow plenty of time to make the change. Look in your rearview and side mirrors to judge the flow of traffic. Be cautious of other drivers in your blind spot. That is the spot that isn't picked up by your mirrors. Always look to the right and left before making a lane change.

- If you encounter a tailgater, just move over to a slower lane until that driver passes you by. Remain calm. Keep anger away from your driving habits.

When Riding the Bus

- Don't be loud or disruptive on a bus, train, or subway. Blaring music or loud cell phone conversations are not a good idea.

- Be polite to the driver, and show your appreciation for their driving you safely to your destination.

- If you see a person running to catch the ride, let drivers know so they can wait for that passenger to board.

- Extend your seat to an elderly person, a disabled person, someone on crutches, or to a pregnant woman. It used to be common practice to extend these courtesies, but people seem to be focused on themselves much of the time. Be polite. Extend these same manners today.

- Be willing to help someone with their luggage if they need help.

The Big Screen Scene

- Be on time so you don't have to crawl over or bump people as you take your seat.

- Silence is a virtue once the performance has started. The sound of someone chewing popcorn, cracking gum, or rattling candy wrappers is very annoying during a show. Don't let your behavior disturb those around you.

- If you have to get up from your seat before the performance is over, be sure you exit with a minimum of distraction. Whisper "excuse me" as you step around people.

- When entering a filled row, face the people as you tread

down to your seat. It's better to see your face than your backside. Also use "excuse me."

- Leave the area around you clean. Take with you the empty beverage cup, the candy wrappers, and the empty popcorn boxes.

While at the Market

- Remember to control your children. Unruly children are a big distraction for other shoppers. They aren't too pleasant for you either.

- If you see food items knocked off the shelf or positioned on the floor, take time to pick them up and place them back in the proper position on the shelf.

- Be careful as you turn the corners at the end of the aisles. There might be oncoming traffic.

- Be sensitive when you're checking out with a basketful of groceries. You might let the person behind you with a few items go ahead of you.

- Use the quick checkout register when you meet the qualifications (10 to 12 items only).

- Be friendly to the checkout employees. Get to know them— it's nice to develop a friendship with people you encounter daily or at least weekly.

- If someone assists you with your bags out to the parking lot, give them a big thank-you.

- Recycle your plastic or paper bags. It helps a little with the landfill, and it will be a savings to the cost of the grocery store.

- Return your shopping cart back to the proper storage location for your carts. Many cars are dented because of carts left in the wrong place. The next dent might be yours.

When Recreating

There's nothing like getting out of the city and into a tranquil mountain or beach area. After only a few hours in a relaxing setting, our bodies and spirits tell us that we need this change in our lives. People who favor the outdoors typically extend courtesies to nature and to other people who enjoy these escapes.

• Whenever you leave such an area, it should look better than when you arrived. Pick up every piece of waste and extinguish any embers in the fire ring.

• Control the sound level of your radios and TV. You might enjoy your choice of sound, but your neighbor may have different preferences.

• If you're at the beach and riding waves on a board, watch for people around you. It's rude, not to mention dangerous, to crash into a swimmer because you haven't taken the time to be sure your path is clear.

• While boating, always have someone in the boat on the alert for swimmers and other boaters. Boating and alcohol don't mix.

• Take time to teach your children how to properly take care of the outdoors. They will often imitate what they see and hear you do.

At Poolside

• If you don't have a pool, be courteous and wait for an invitation. Don't expect to be invited to your friends' pool just because it's a beautiful, sunny day. Respect that your friend might want a quiet afternoon around her pool alone.

• An invitation to swim doesn't mean you have an invitation to use the people's home, their phone, their TV, their indoor restroom, or their refrigerator. Be sure to ask permission before using anything other than their pool.

- Don't overstay your time at the pool unless the host invites you for a longer period of time.

- If a shower is available, take a shower before entering the pool. Your body sweat, sunscreen, and tanning oils affect the chemicals in the pool.

- Offer to bring your own towels. Don't expect your host to furnish your towels.

- Bring along some snacks and beverages for the day.

- Check to be sure others around you are okay with noise before you start splashing or playing Marco Polo.

- If children are invited, you become their lifeguard. Don't expect the host to be responsible for their safety.

- Control the behavior and manners of your kids. No host wants to see their landscaping trampled or chlorine dripped all over their blooming plants. Remember the Golden Rule.

With Those Who Serve You

We occasionally must use the services of professionals who serve us, such as a doctor, dentist, lawyer, or financial advisor. If we treat them with proper respect, they will give us better service, and we can establish a longer and better working relationship.

- Respect who they are and their expertise.

- Even though you pay for such services, it's nice to let them know that you appreciate all that they do to help you with your situation.

- Remember to make the encounter a win-win experience. You get proper help and they get a good client.

- A thank-you note is appropriate to express your joy in working with them.

- Be on time for your appointments. Time is money for the professional.

- Don't take advantage of professionals who are also your personal friends. If they perform a service for you, be sure to offer payment for their services.

- Professionals are often cornered at social functions and asked for free advice. If you need their advice, call their office and set up an appointment.

The Repairman

We don't live in a caste system. All of us need to be treated with dignity and with respect. Treat tradesmen with proper respect. Here are a few ideas:

- Don't talk down to them or make rude commands.

- Welcome them with a friendly hello when they arrive on the scene. They are going to solve your problem. It might be a clogged drain, a darkened TV, a light switch that doesn't work, or a stalled automobile.

- Get to know the person's name and refer to it. It's always better for them to hear their name rather than "Hey you." First names go a long way.

- Be specific in stating what and where your problem is.

- Give respect to the helpers. They are people who are as important as you are.

- Put workers at ease when they arrive. Talk about sports, the weather, their families, and the like. Make them feel comfortable. Depending on the situation you might offer a glass of iced tea, a cup of coffee, or even a soft drink.

- When the repair is completed, give a warm and heartfelt thank-you.

- If you're really pleased with the work, take time to send a

note of appreciation to the company, stating that the trades-
man did a fine job while at your home or office.

- When you receive good service, consider spreading positive
  word of mouth to friends and neighbors to help the business.

*It is not what he has, nor even what he does, which
directly expresses the worth of a man, but what he is.*

—Henri-Frederic Amiel

Good Manners Even in Death

As a well-spent day brings happy sleep,
so a life well used brings happy death.

—Leonardo da Vinci

We and our family members will all experience that last rite of passage—death. When someone in your family or a close friend passes away, someone must step up to the plate and take charge. This person must be very sensitive that the remaining family members are helped and that final funeral arrangements are carried out.

This difficult time requires us to see to it that family members are consoled while many details are being taken care of. If you are the take-charge person, you will be responsible for the overall smooth coordination of the funeral and the interment. Here are some pointers that might be of assistance to someone who is taking on this responsibility:

- Make a checklist of what needs to be done.

- Delegate some of these jobs to various family members and close friends.

- Remember to include in your list the specific desires that the deceased may have requested.

- If small children are involved, identify a family who would be willing to house, feed, and take care of their needs for the next four or five days. This can be done in your own home, or they may need to go to a host family's home.

- A very important volunteer is the person or team of persons to handle the necessary calls of the home of the deceased. This is a very demanding responsibility. All family members need to be notified and given all the particulars about the events of the next few days. If the person is still employed, the place of employment needs to be notified. This team or person will handle all of the communication of information concerning the events leading up to and including the funeral services.

- Immediately notify the deceased person's lawyer, insurance agent, and accountant.

- Notify the funeral home and deal with the details that are necessary to plan and organize.

  - Arrange a viewing or wake.

  - Select the casket and plot if that hasn't been pre-arranged.

  - Decide on the burial clothes.

  - Coordinate burial plans with the church and cemetery.

- Designate someone who will be in charge of feeding everyone staying at the home of the departed.

- Appoint someone else to be in charge of handling the reception after the services. Identify when that event will take place. It might be at the home of the deceased, in a church fellowship hall, at a country club, or at a hotel conference ballroom. Remember to invite these people:

  - members of the immediate family

  - the minister, priest, or rabbi in charge of the service

  - ushers and honorary pallbearers

- – close social and business friends
- – out-of-town guests
- Another person needs to handle all other correspondence and records such as these:
  - – e-mails
  - – sympathy cards to the family
  - – records of who sent flowers for future thank-you cards
  - – logs of those who brought food, beverages, and gifts
- Another person is needed who will make these arrangements for all out-of-town guests:
  - – Make hotel reservations.
  - – Track plane arrivals if transportation is needed.
  - – Help with meals while visitors are in town.
  - – Make sure these guests get back to the airport.
- Notify the newspapers to have a death notice included in the earliest edition. The mortuary can often assist you with this detail.

What Words Need to be Said

Most people are usually at a loss for words when talking to the family members of someone who has just passed away. Here are a few suggestions:

- Talk about what a wonderful person the deceased was. Recount a personal story you can share.
- Discuss how much you loved this person and what a personal loss you feel.
- Mention how sorry you were to learn of this sad news.
- Describe how much you will grieve for the family left behind.

- Express how much the deceased will be missed by friends and colleagues.

What About Flowers?

The family will usually make their wishes known about flower contributions. More and more people are not requesting flowers but are suggesting that friends and others contribute on behalf of the deceased and their family to a favorite, specified charity. Also, various religious denominations have certain guidelines regarding the display of flowers at their funerals.

- Flowers are never sent for a Jewish funeral. They will often recommend a favorite charity.

- Only a spray of flowers for the top of the casket from the family is protocol for those of the Catholic faith.

- In Protestant churches, flowers are permitted on and near the altar.

If flowers are sent to the funeral home, they will be transferred to the graveside on the day of the funeral.

Proper Dress for the Funeral

In more formal times of history, widows dressed in black mourning attire. Even today, at funerals for high state and national figures, the widow dresses in a black dress, black hat, black gloves, and even a black veil. For most funerals, however, the widow should be dressed discreetly in a dark dress or suit.

- The small children of the deceased should be properly dressed for the occasion. For the girls it would include a nice dress and appropriate shoes. Little boys would dress in a suit with white shirt and matching tie, with neatly polished shoes.

- Older children and grown children should wear appropriately simple clothing.

- Young men and grown sons should dress as the ushers and pallbearers do—in dark suits, white shirt, dark tie, and dark shoes.

- Friends and colleagues should be dressed in quiet clothing. Now is not the time or occasion to wear your flashy and colorful outfits. Downplay your dress. After all, you're honoring the deceased with your presence.

The Church Service

Each denomination of faith will have its own format for the service. Many churches today have "celebration services" to honor and remember the life of the deceased. With a small gathering, it could be short and simple, and with a larger gathering it could include video productions on the large screen. Several friends and family members could participate in giving the eulogy. The music could be simple or very extensive, including some of the deceased person's favorite hymns, a song from a soloist, and even a few congregational songs.

You as a family can determine what will be included in your church service—some families may even decide that they will not have a church service, but the immediate family and a few close friends will have a short graveside ceremony.

A Cremation

With the increasing costs related to having a traditional burial of loved ones, many families are choosing to have the deceased cremated. A cremation is usually preceded by a memorial funeral service in a church. Only a few relatives and close friends go to the crematorium service. The ashes are then given to the family and dispersed by them in a manner selected in their deceased family member's will. Sometimes they are placed in an urn and then kept at the family burial plot. Depending on your state law you may or may not scatter the ashes in other settings. Check with the mortuary to see what your state requires.

The Follow-Up

The time leading up to the funeral creates a lot of activity and excitement. Friends and family are over, food is being served, hugs are abundant, tears flow, and there is a lot of comfort. But after the funeral, everyone goes home, the phone doesn't ring as much, and the support is no longer there. We need to follow up and give continued support—let them know we have not forgotten them. Call them. Invite them to breakfast, lunch, or dinner. Send a card letting them know that you are thinking of them. Keep in contact. It will be so encouraging to those who have lost that loved one. They will soon forget the flowers you sent, but they will never forget the love and support you give after the passing of that loved one. Stay in touch.

In my Father's house are many rooms; if it were not so, I would have told you. I am going there to prepare a place for you. And if I go and prepare a place for you, I will come back and take you to be with me that you also may be where I am.

—John 14:2-3

Notes

Chapter 4—The Manners of Invitation

1. Emile Barnes, *The Twelve Teas of Friendship* (Eugene, OR: Harvest House Publishers, 2001), pp. 10-11.

Chapter 6—Tips on Tipping

1. Currently a good source for information on proper tipping is *http://www.fairtip.org.*

Chapter 17—Communication from Afar

1. Lynne Brennan, *Business Etiquette for the 21st Century* (London: Piatkus Books LTD, 2003), pp. 76-77.

Chapter 19—Five Manners Most Parents Forget to Teach

1. Mary Mohler, "5 Manners Most Parents Forget to Teach," *Family Circle Magazine,* March 12, 2002.

2. A Donna Otto resource as taught at her "Youniquely Woman Seminar." Used by permission.

Chapter 24—The Art of Helping

1. Lauren Littauer Briggs, *The Art of Helping* (Colorado Springs, CO: RiverOak Publishing, 2003), p. 123. Used by permission.

2. Ibid., p. 124.

Chapter 25—The Etiquette of Caring

1. Lauren Littauer Briggs, *The Art of Helping* (Colorado Springs, CO: RiverOak Publishing, 2003), pp. 17-26. Used by permission.

2. Ibid., pp. 15-16.

Chapter 27—The Art of Conversation

1. Margaret Shepherd, *The Art of Civilized Conversation* (New York, NY: Broadway Books, 2005), p. 16.

Chapter 29—A Tea Party Has Its Own Etiquette

1. Adapted from Emilie Barnes and Anne Christian Buchanan, *Everything I Know I Learned Over Tea* (Eugene, OR: Harvest House Publishers, 2004), pp. 47-48.

192 🜚 Good Manners *for* $\mathcal{E}$*very* $\mathcal{O}$*ccasion*

Chapter 30—Wediquette Etiquette: Part I

1. Yetta Fisher Gruen, *Wediquette* (New York, NY: Penguin Books USA Inc., 1995). Taken from the title of her book.

Chapter 31—Wediquette Etiquette: Part II

1. Adapted from Yetta Fisher Gruen, *Wediquette* (New York, NY: Penguin Books USA Inc., 1995), pp. 130-32.

Chapter 32—Being a Gracious Adult

1. A Donna Otto resource, Homemakers by Choice, Scottsdale, Arizona, 2007. Used by permission.